THE CHRONICLES OF A COURTIER

The Stanton Courtiers 2005
Back row, left to right: Alex and Sarah Greig, The Old Pantry; Tim, Marina, Georgina and Victoria Cowan, Stables Cottage; Paul Rosser, Jo Gingell, Isabella and Amelia Rosser, West Wing
Front row, left to right: Jeanine, Celina and Denis Goddard, the Coach House; Peter, Fiona and Beatrice Baskett with Pongo the labrador, Stanton Court; Rachel Clark and Nigel Fleet, North Wing

The Chronicles of a Courtier

A HISTORY OF STANTON COURT
WILTSHIRE

Fiona Gilroy Baskett

To Heather,
with love and best wishes
Fiona Gilroy Baskett x.

FOR BEATRICE

First published in the United Kingdom in 2006 by The Hobnob Press, PO Box 1838, East Knoyle, Salisbury SP3 6FA

British Library Cataloguing in Publication Data
A catalogue record for this book is available from the British Library.

ISBN 0-946418-44-6

Typeset in 11/15 pt Scala
Typesetting and origination by John Chandler
Printed in Great Britain by Salisbury Printing Company Ltd, Salisbury

Contents

Foreword by
His Grace the Duke of Beaufort

Fortunately rural England is still alive and well and retains many of its original villages, albeit developed to accommodate modern times. The key features of most villages in the 17th and 18th centuries were the Church, the Rectory, the Manor House, the farm and the homes of those who worked locally. In the early part of the 20th century this tradition faded and the Church found it difficult and expensive to maintain large properties and equip them with modern amenities such as electricity and mains water. Consequently many rectories passed into private hands and became family homes. These days the majority of village residents earn their living outside the village and rarely are houses, and their history, passed from generation to generation.

Stanton St. Quintin, North Wiltshire, in the heart of Beaufort Hunt country, is just one of these villages. The village developed around the 12th-century church which still acts as the hub for many in the community. The original rectory, constructed from local Cotswold stone, was built in 1780 and passed into private hands in the 1920s. The present occupant Fiona Gilroy Baskett has researched and recorded the history of the house, and most importantly the characters who have lived there for the past two and a half centuries. Over that time much has changed in the fabric but the stories of those who lived there continue to thrive.

I have so enjoyed reading this book and the descriptions of the people and places, many of whom I have been lucky enough to have met over the years, and feel most honoured to have been asked to write this short foreword.

Beaufort.
Badminton, January 2006.

Introduction

'To excel the past we must not allow ourselves to lose contact with it; on the contrary, we must feel it under our feet because we raised ourselves upon it.'
José Ortega Y Gasset

Visitors to Stanton Court often ask me about the history of the house. Moving here in 1996 there were many features that intrigued me – the detailed inscriptions surmounting the heavy wooden front door, the panelled sitting room, the imposing yew avenue to the south of the house and the secret passage in the cellar. However it is not merely bricks and mortar which interest me, rather the inhabitants who have made their mark here, and I resolved that one day I would find out more about the people who lived at the Court in an era spanning over two hundred years.

What soon became apparent in my quest for more information was that the history of Stanton Court is inextricably linked to its parish. The present house was built as a Rectory in 1780 and was owned by the Church for over 140 years, eventually being sold by the Bishop of Bristol in 1924. It then passed into private ownership and acquired a variety of roles including a residence for the gentry and occasional sanctum for the Royal Family, a billet for the WAAFs in World War II, and a school.

The ensuing account of life at Stanton Court therefore is interspersed liberally with vignettes of local history, which in many cases are by no means complete, but which I hope will paint a picture of the people who have shaped the history of the Court.

Throughout the book the Court is referred to variously as Stanton Rectory, Rectory House and Stanton Court, and all are one and the same place.

It was both pertinent and exciting to find that two of Wiltshire's finest antiquarians, John Aubrey and Canon Jackson lived locally, and were contemporaries and acquaintances of Rev. John Byrom and Rev. Hon. Bertrand Bouverie respectively, both of whom were Rectors of St. Giles Church, Stanton St. Quintin.

John Aubrey, who was born in Kington St. Michael in 1625, wrote the manuscripts which comprise his *Natural History of Wiltshire* between 1656 and 1691, and this work was later edited by John Britton and published by the Wiltshire Topographical Society in 1847. His *Wiltshire Collections*, written between 1659 and 1670, were annotated around two hundred years later by Canon J.E. Jackson and published as Aubrey's *Topographical Collections for Wiltshire* in 1862.

Canon Jackson was Rector of Leigh Delamere in 1845 and also held the position of archivist to the 4th Marquis of Bath. He amassed an extensive archive of Wiltshire history, some of which was bequeathed to the Wiltshire Archaeological and Natural History Museum in Devizes and some to the Society of Antiquaries of London. He died at Leigh Delamere in 1891. Much of the early history of Stanton Court comes from the extensive collections of these renowned historians.

There are many people who have helped me along this historical journey and to these people I offer my sincere thanks.

I thank His Grace the Duke of Beaufort for providing the foreword for this book, for which I am most grateful.

I would also like to thank local historian Countess June Badeni who has encouraged me to turn this rainy day pastime into an absorbing study in antiquities. Her knowledge and guidance have been inspirational, and as a result my enquiries have spread not only across Wiltshire and Britain, but far overseas.

My thanks are due also to Elizabeth Gibb, who has shared willingly her extensive knowledge of village history with me, Capt. John Cannan and Mrs Helen McAlpine (née Cannan), Simon Spicer, John Spicer, Gillian Howard, Betty Boast, Frank Randall, Bernard and Elizabeth Anstee, Angela Smith, Maureen Smith, Philip and Elizabeth Bullock, Duncan and Linda Hickling, Keith and Audrey Galpin, Pam Iles, Shirley Cooper, Sarah Miles, Sue Love, Anne and Paul Adams. I am also grateful to John Williams, David Emeney and Margaret MacGregor of the Bristol Record Office, Martyn Henderson of the Wiltshire and Swindon Record Office, Yvonne Oliver of the Imperial War Museum, Sophie Gordon, curator of the Royal Photographic Collection, Windsor Castle, David Taylor of the National

Maritime Museum, and staff of the Wiltshire Heritage Museum in Devizes and the Society of Antiquaries of London, all of whom have been most helpful.

Thank you to my publisher, John Chandler, of Hobnob Press, for his guidance, and for allowing me to realise an ambition by seeing this book through to fruition.

Thank you also to Andy Lim for his superb technical assistance over many hours and without whom this book would not have been possible; to my husband, Peter, for his support; and to my neighbours, the Stanton Courtiers, past and present, for their conviviality over the years.

I leave the last word to the Rev. Hon. Bertrand Pleydell Bouverie, Rector of St.Giles from 1870 to 1880. He was, by all accounts, a colourful character, whose indelible style is found throughout Stanton Court. During the course of my research I came across his original diary in which he wrote, in 1877:

> In these days when the inhabitants of our rural parishes are continually migrating, and no longer are there any to be found who have remained in the same parish for more than 1 or 2 generations, I think that unless some record be kept of the traditions and tales concerning such parishes there is great danger that they will soon be lost.
>
> Therefore hoping that it may hereafter be interesting and for some persons who come here hereafter I propose to write down and deposit in the Parish Church this book containing all I have ever heard about the place.

The account which follows, I hope, will do justice to the spirit of continuing this tradition.

Fiona Gilroy Baskett
Stanton Court,
March 2006

1

In the Beginning

Everything has already begun before, the first line of the first page of every novel refers to something that has already happened outside the book.
If on a Winter's Night a Traveller *by Italo Calvino 1979*

One summer's day in 1874, the Rev. Hon. Bertrand Bouverie, Rector of St. Giles, strode across the fields from Stanton Rectory to deliver an urgent message to his friend Canon J.E. Jackson, Rector of Leigh Delamere:

> My Dear Canon,
> I touch this learned cleric with awe!
>
> My brother and I have walked over thinking perhaps to catch you before you started at Stanton Drew.
>
> I have been making an earth for foxes in the wood and in digging it out we have come on to a very curious structure. As yet we have excavated a very small portion and not as yet before the flooring-stones which are set upright, foundations, lots of bones and pottery.
>
> Will you come and lunch with us tomorrow and we will have an archaeological search? J.E. must make it out.
> Yours very faithfully,
> B.P.Bouverie.

And so it was, the following day, that the enthusiastic amateur archaeologist joined forces with the eminent historian, and together they partially excavated the foundations of a Roman villa in Stanton Park, firmly establishing the Romans as the first settlers to put Stanton St. Quintin on the map over two thousand years ago.

Further archaeological sorties in the parish were equally productive. Canon Jackson refers to another Roman settlement uncovered near Clanville:

> An appearance of a Romano-British residence with uneven surface of ground near it, just above a Quarry near Malmesbury road and Clanville. A coin of Constantine, a perfect quern (one stone of it) samian pottery and black pottery found June 1874.

And in 1924 Betrand Bouverie donated some Roman artefacts to the Wiltshire Archaeological and Natural History Museum, accompanied by the following note:

> I send you a fibula [Roman brooch in the form of a safety-pin] and also a glass tear drop found at the same time. It was in some year between 1870 and 1880.I was poking about in a quarry between Upper and Lower Stanton when I saw what I believed was a cinerary urn of red brown pottery among the stones. I tried to get it out but unfortunately it fell to pieces so small that I could not put it together again, but in it I found this fibula and also the tear drop. When I got them the pin was still in the brooch but it was so rusted at the point that it fell off and alas I have lost it. I can't make out what the metal is made of.

The objects in question, now housed in the Devizes museum, originated from a Roman burial site in Stanton.

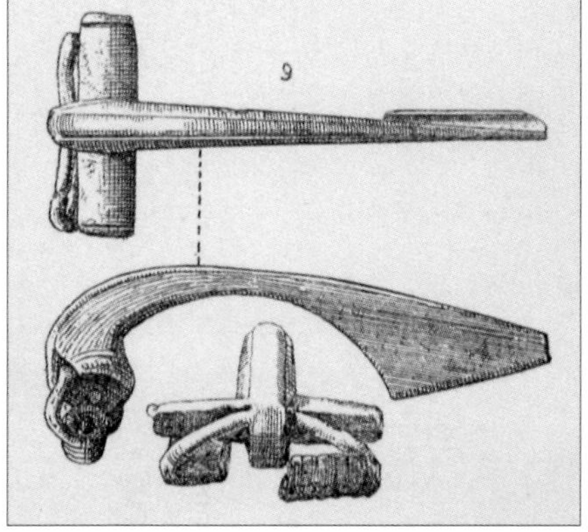

Fibula from Woodcutts similar to the one found by Bouverie (Pitt-Rivers, Cranborne Chase *1, pl.xii (9)*

It should come as no surprise that even two thousand years ago a '*des res*' in Stanton St. Quintin had appeal. One has only to look at a modern map to realise that the Roman settlement at Stanton lay equidistant between the prosperous garrison town of *Corinium* (Cirencester) to the north and the religious spa and cultural centre of *Aquae Sulis* (Bath) to the South West and these two centres were linked by the Fosse Way, a remarkable road which ran a direct course for 182 miles from Lincoln to South Petherton in Somerset passing through Sherston and Grittleton en route.

Much later our knowledge of the area comes from the Anglo-Saxon period. In 642 A.D. an Irish monk named Mailduib established a hermitage which gradually grew into the settlement of Malmesbury, five miles from Stanton. A young monk named Aldhelm came to study under him and founded a monastery in 676 A.D. This became a centre of pilgrimage and an Abbey was built on this spot in the 12th century.

Aldhelm was a charismatic figure who was reported to have miraculous powers and he was later consecrated a saint. In 705 A.D. he left Malmesbury to be consecrated as Bishop of Sherborne and 1300 years later the anniversary of this event is still commemorated in Malmesbury. At the end of the ninth century the town was included in a list of boroughs fortified during Alfred's reign.

Alfred's grandson was King Athelstan, considered by some to be the first king of all England. Given his supreme importance in European history it is remarkable that he was in fact a local lad. Between 925 and 940 A.D. King

Athelstan's tomb in Malmesbury Abbey (reproduced with kind permission of Woodmansterne Publications Ltd)

Athelstan reigned over a huge kingdom, of which Malmesbury was his capital. He later forged European alliances by marrying off four of his half sisters to various Western European rulers.

King Athelstan died in 940 A.D. and he was buried in Malmesbury Abbey. Although his tomb can be found in the North aisle, it stands empty as the King's relics, which were originally buried in the east end of the abbey, disappeared around 1539 when the monastery was dissolved. Athelstan had been a notable supporter of the Abbey endowing it with artworks and religious relics. His gifts included a gold cross with a relic of the True Cross which he used to wear in his battles and numerous relics of saints purchased from abroad.

It is known that King Athelstan conferred privileges of five 'hides' (perhaps equivalent to 600 acres) of land near Norton to men who helped him in his campaigns against the Danes, and according to the scholar William of Malmesbury (1095-1142) Athelstan gave a large number of estates to the Abbey.

Some of the neighbouring places which grew around Stanton St. Quintin, such as Corston, originally belonged to Malmesbury Abbey; however we know that from the mid-13th century the overlordship of Stanton Manor was known as part of the honour of Gloucester .

Our earliest written history of the parish comes from the 11th century Domesday Book, in which the area now known as Stanton St. Quintin, is referred to as *Stantone*, meaning 'stone farm'.

On the orders of King William I, in 1086, royal commissioners conducted an extensive property survey of the English shires. This survey listed the names of landholders, their status, the size of their holding and its use, its tax liability and the number of animals it supported. The information, collectively known as the Domesday Book, was used to maximise revenue for the Normans in a system which may find parallels with many contemporary councils.

The Domesday Book comprises two volumes – Little Domesday covering Norfolk, Suffolk and Essex, and Great Domesday covering the rest of England except the four northern shires and London and Winchester, from which the following extract is taken:

> Osbern holds Stantone himself. Brictic held it before 1066; it paid tax for 18 hides. He has 2 ploughs in Lordship on 9 hides. 7 slaves there. 9 villagers and 3 cottages with 6 ploughs; meadow 6 acres; pasture 1 league long and 1 wide; woodland 1 league long and 3 furlongs wide. The value was £9. now £8

It is also known, from other Domesday extracts, that the Brictic referred to here was leased land in Stanton from the Abbots of Glastonbury: 'In Stanton (St.Quintin) the Abbot of Glastonbury leased 6 acres of meadow to Brictic before 1066. Osbern Gifford holds them now'. And as will be revealed later there is evidence linking the Abbots of Glastonbury with Stanton Court as it stands today.

The suffix St. Quintin which was added to the name Stanton in the 13th century derives from the St. Quintin family who were Lords of the Manor circa 1210-50. The Fitzhugh family succeeded the St. Quintin family, and were related by marriage, residing as Lords of the Manor from the late 13th to 15th century and some early deeds also refer to the parish as Stanton Fitzhugh.

From as early as the 11th century the parish has consisted of two different villages. In 1223 these were known as Stanton, which was the site of the church, manor house and parsonage, and Nether Stanton, the site of the tenantry farmsteads and later a nonconformist chapel. Stanton later became Upper Stanton and hundreds of years later the two parts of the parish, separated by

The inscription above Stanton Court front door (photograph by author)

the main Chippenham–Malmesbury Road became Stanton St. Quintin and Lower Stanton St. Quintin..

Observant visitors to Stanton Court today must cast their eyes upwards above the stone porch entrance. Encased in stone above the heavy oak front door are the initials S.S. 1780, which refer to the Rev. Samuel Smith, who built the present rectory in 1780. Surmounting the initials are three stone shields which are all that remain of the original parsonage which was destroyed in the 17th century.

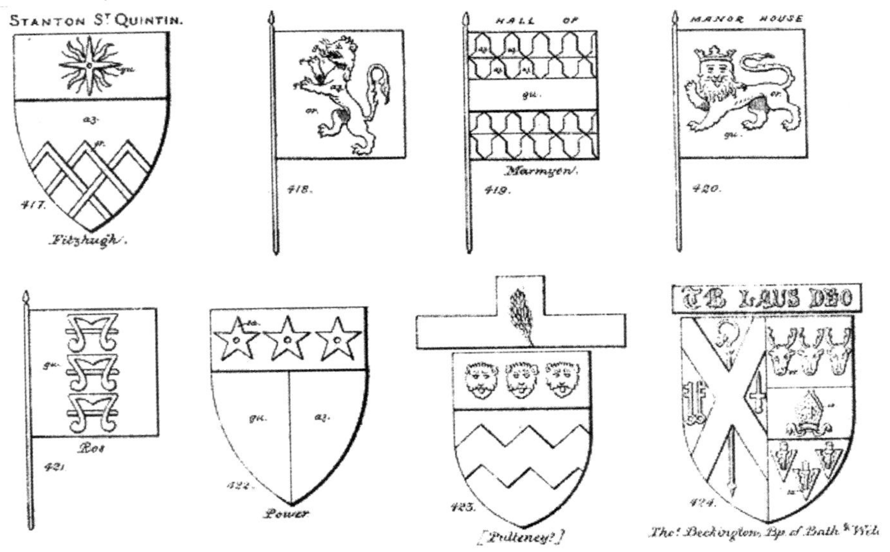

Stanton coats of arms, from Aubrey's Wiltshire Collections.

The central shield is the See of Wells which is surmounted by the inscription 'T.B. Laus Deo'. T.B. refers to Thomas Beckington, the Bishop of Wells who died in 1464 and whom we know had connections with the St. Quintin family, as his coat of arms is also found in the chancel window at Hinton St. George where one of the St. Quintin family was buried.

The shield on the left, consisting of three interlocking chevronels is that of the Fitzhugh family, patrons in the 13th, 14th and 15th centuries. The third shield, according to Canon Jackson, represents the patronage of Richard Beere, the last but one of the Abbots of Glastonbury A.D. 1493-1524. It is this third shield which provides the link between Stanton Court today and the ancient monastic order of one thousand years ago.

2
Debauchery, Robbery and Murder most Foul

In my own district once there used to be
A fine archdeacon, one of high degree,
Who boldly did the execution due
On fornication and on witchcraft too,
Bawdry, adultery and defamation,
Breaches of wills and contract, spoliation
Of church endowment, failure in the rents
And tithes, and disregard of sacraments,
All these and many other kinds of crime
That need have no rehearsal at this time,
Usury, simony too. But he could boast
That lechery was what he punished most.'

'The Friar's Tale' from The Canterbury Tales *by Geoffrey Chaucer c.1387*

Throughout the ages the history of Stanton Court, formerly the Rectory, has become inextricably linked with that of St. Giles Church and the Manor House, because traditionally the right to present Rectors of the Church descended with the lordship of Stanton St. Quintin Manor.

This patronage existed from Norman times right through to the Earls of Radnor at the beginning of the 20th century. The parish of Pewsey was also in the living of the Radnor family and both Frederick Pleydell Bouverie and Bertrand Pleydell Bouverie, sons of the 2nd and 4th Earls of Radnor respectively, served as Rectors in both parishes. Appendix 1 (page 89) details the incumbency of the Parish from the 13th century until 1780 when the Rectory now known as Stanton Court was built.

In 1507 the patron is named as His Majesty the King (Henry VII) because George Fitzhugh was a minor. In 1609 the King (this time James I of England) once again presented *per lapsum.*

Early church records name Matthew Hamme as the first rector in 1296 and in 1300 he received a licence to visit Rome. From 1312 a vicar was ordained to serve the church with the rector and this appears to have continued until 1434 when the vicarage was consolidated with the rectory following a petition from the then rector who claimed that the church's income had declined and was then too small for two incumbents.

During the reign of the Plantagenet king Edward I, Stanton Manor was the residence of Sir Herbert de St. Quentin and he appointed Matthew Hamme's successor, Edgar de Wyly in 1302.

Print of watercolour of St. Giles Church, by John Buckler, 1808 (Wilts C.C. P43307)

Figure of Christ triumphing over the dragon, below west window (photograph by author)

Over the next 100 years many short incumbencies followed, the most notable of which appears to have been Nicholas Sterre, a carousing Rector, who in 1410, was accused of frequenting taverns and who was also accused, but found not guilty, of being absent from the Church and of adultery.

The Norman Church in Stanton St. Quintin was built in the 12th century and became dedicated in 1763 to St. Giles, an 8th-century abbot from Provence. Fine examples of Norman work exist in the central tower, which inside is supported by a finely cut zig-zag arch, in the rounded nave arcade and font, and in a sculptured figure of Christ triumphing over the dragon, which can be found outside under the west window. The South doorway of the church is another of the many examples of entrances being placed on the side furthest from the village, again a Norman characteristic.

Observers with keen eyesight may be able to spot an unusual second sculpture, an explicitly female figure, very high up on the exterior north wall of the church tower. This is known by the Irish name of sheela-na-gig. It is possible that such carvings were fertility symbols or that they were intended as protecting charms to ward off evil or as a warning against sexual licence. The only other similar sculptures of this nature to be found in Wiltshire are at Oaksey and Devizes.

The aisle was added circa 1200 as was the small vestry which was probably originally built as a chapel. In the 15th century

Sheela-na-gig. North wall of church tower (photograph by author)

Stained glass window of St. Matthew (photograph by author)

a new west window and two north windows were inserted in the nave. One of the north stained glass windows depicts St. Matthew. Assiduous study of the detail in this picture reveals Matthew to have six toes!

The Church was formerly collegiate and Aubrey mentions two old collegiate seats for priests and boxes for their song books in the chancel which were in evidence in Aubrey's time around 1670. Further restorations and additions were made in the 19th and 20th centuries and these are considered in a later chapter.

It is thought that prior to 1780 when Stanton Court was built, a glebe house, or parsonage, belonging to the Church had stood on this same site since the early 16th century. John Aubrey records that the Parsonage had a fine hall with much painted glass in the windows and coats of arms with mitres, and that on the porch of the hall were three coats of arms well carved in stone. It is these three inscriptions that were reset over the door of new rectory where they still remain to this day.

The Church Survey in Wiltshire 1649-50 states that: 'Stanton St. Quintin is a parsonage valued att one hundred pounds per annum and the Church landes att six shillings per annum.'

From the 16th century most rectors seemed to have lived in the parish and to have served the parish themselves without the assistance of a curate. This trend has been reversed in the 21st century, which has seen the Rev. Andrew Evans, Rector, made an Honorary Canon of the Diocese of Bristol, and St. Giles Church becoming one of eight churches in the Gauzebrook Area Ministry, assisted by two curates.

Rev. John Byrom M.A. (1648-1717), fellow of King's College, Cambridge, was presented to Stanton Rectory in 1677 by Sir Giles Hungerford of Coulston, a position which he held for 40 years. The glebe land at Stanton St. Quintin during his incumbency consisted of 135 acres.

Regretably, in 1693, he was the victim of a robbery at Stanton Rectory which he recounted in a letter to Bishop Tanner:

> [I] had been apprehending all the winter that my house would be broken open: which was done last night. The villains extremely surprised me by coming at such an hour with drawn swords. They eased me of my money, plate, linen to the value of £20, and put me into such a fright which I have hardly recovered.

Thankfully he did recover and went on to serve the parish for another 24 years. When he died he was buried at West Lavington (where his father Thomas Byrom had been vicar for some years).

In his *Natural History of Wiltshire*, John Aubrey recalls the Manor House and the Rectory during the incumbency of Rev. John Byrom: 'In the Parish of Stanton St. Quintin are but twenty three houses and when Mr. Byrom was inducted, 1677, here were 8 persons of 80 years of age.'

He goes on to provide an evocative description of the characteristics of the Manor House in the late 17th century, which at that time was occupied by Sir Giles Hungerford:

John Aubrey, engraving from his Wiltshire Collections

> Heretofore all gentlemen's houses had fish ponds, and then houses had motes drawn about them, both for strength and for convenience of fish on fasting days.
>
> The architecture of an old English gentleman's house, especially in Wiltshire and thereabout, was a good high strong wall, a gatehouse. A great hall and parlour, and within the little green court where you come in stood on one side the barne; they then thought not the noise of the threshold ill musique. This is yet to be seen at severall old houses and seats e.g. Bradfield, Alderton, Stanton St. Quintin, Yatton Keynell etc.

Upon Rev. John Byrom's death in 1717 the Rev. William Twentyman was appointed Rector by Sir Giles Hungerford's son-in-law, Lord Robert Lexington, to whom he had been chaplain at Madrid.

It was during his incumbency that a notorious crime took place in Stanton Park – a heinous murder, the story of which has been passed down through the centuries.

In 1764 two sailors were paid off from the Royal Naval vessel *HMS Stag*. No one is sure exactly where they came from – either London or Porstmouth – but it is thought they were on their way to Bristol via the old 'wagon road', which passed through Stanton St. Quintin, Grittleton, Tolldown and Pucklechurch, to board a ship bound for the West Indies.

On disembarking from *HMS Stag* they had both been paid £28 and they proceeded to fritter this away in the local hostelries. One of the sailors, William Jacques, was the delinquent son of Henry Jacques who was Rector of Leigh Delamere from 1752 to 1786. He met up with his fellow shipmate, the negro George Hartford, in the 'Green Dragon Inn' in Malmesbury and they engaged on a pub crawl together, also visiting the 'White Lion' and the 'Prince and Princess'. Having lodged at the latter inn they were definitely the worse for wear and got into a fight at Malmesbury Cross when Bill Jacques, who had lost his purse, accused Hartford of stealing it. The local constable tried to persuade the two men to leave town at the instigation of the High Steward of Malmesbury, a Mr. Wilkins. One of the reasons given for this was that if a murder was committed in the town the burgers would lose the right to send Members to Parliament and the commoners would lose their right to the Common.

Even when they got to Town Bridge Jacques tried to push Hartford into Mill Pond and they continued quarrelling along the Corston road, frightening the villagers. They eventually parted company in Stanton. Jacques stayed in the village to get some food, telling the locals he had been robbed whilst Hartford proceeded along the road into Stanton Park then sat down and went to sleep at a place known as the Black Pond, not far from the site of the Roman villa. Eventually Jacques caught up with him and bludgeoned him to death. Some boys who had been following saw Jacques committing the murder and rifling the other sailor's pockets and they ran back and told a woodman who gathered a group of locals to track down the assailant.

Jacques was followed and arrested in a public house in Chippenham. There was plenty of evidence to incriminate him – his pockets were full of money and he was wearing Hartford's handkerchief round his neck at the time of arrest – and he confessed to the murder. He was tried at Salisbury where he confessed to three other murders as well as a robbery on Hounslow Heath and he was sentenced to death.

His public execution, by hanging, took place on Stanton Common between Upper and Lower Stanton on a site now occupied by the aerodrome. Many people from Malmesbury, Chippenham and the local villages came to observe the execution and the scene was described as resembling a fair with booths and standings.

The execution took place on a clear hot day in September but legend has it that as the culprit was brought to the scaffold a small black cloud appeared over the gibbet and at the moment of death there was a flash of lightning and a thunderstorm erupted in Stanton which lasted all day. None of the surrounding villages was affected.

The gallows and chains remained on Stanton Common for many years and a bush grew at the site of the hanging which became known as Jacques Bush.

Many years later, during the Second World War, a young WAAF billeted at Stanton Court, described her blind terror on returning home from the aerodrome each night whenever she passed a certain tree near the little bridge where the road dips near the Officers' Mess. Her fear became so real and incapacitating that it occupied her nightmares and she resorted to being accompanied home each night. In an attempt to rationalise this fear she related it to her adrenaline fuelled experiences of working as a wartime navigator which she believed had given her a heightened sense of awareness. It wasn't until several years later, on returning to the village, that she learned that the place which had unleashed such fear within her was the site of the hanging tree and only then could she put her ghosts to rest.

George Hartford lies in an unmarked grave in the west side of St. Giles churchyard.

3
A New Rectory for Stanton St. Quintin

Beneath those rugged elms, that yew-tree's shade,
Where heaves the turf in many a mould'ring heap
Each in his narrow cell forever laid,
The rude Forefathers of the hamlet sleep.

from *Elegy in a Country Churchyard* by Thomas Gray (1716-1771)

The late-18th century was the Age of Enlightenment. In 1769, five years after the murder in Stanton Park, Captain James Cook charted the east coast of Australia. In 1774, the same year that James Watt made the first steam engine, ground-breaking discoveries were being made even nearer to home with the discovery of oxygen by Joseph Priestley working in his laboratory at Bowood House, Wiltshire.

Ten miles away, in 1780, Rev. Samuel Smith arrived in Stanton St. Quintin and took up residence in the new Rectory.

Samuel was the son of the wealthy city gent Thomas Smith of Salisbury and a graduate of Trinity College, Oxford. His wealth was partly reflected in the scale of his rectory which at that time consisted of a substantial double pile stone house of three storeys, including three attic dormers, plus cellars. This building forms the central part of Stanton Court today, although the dormers have been replaced by two gables and several wings and outbuildings were subsequently added.

It is also interesting to note that in Samuel Smith's time the main entrance to the house was on the south side, although the impressive yew avenue which exists today was a 20th-century addition. The inscription which surmounts the front door of Stanton Court incorporates Samuel Smith's initials together with three shields which were brought from the original parsonage (described in Chapter 1).

In 1783 Samuel Smith also became Rector of Hardenhuish. He held a service in Stanton St. Quintin every Sunday and celebrated communion three times a year. At that time there were only eight communicants in the parish.

During his incumbency he tried unsuccessfully to start a little school in the village. In 1818 church records state that the population of the parish was 216 and:

> an old woman has a school for the poor children at which about 6 or 7 generally attend. Almost all the poor are relieved by the parish, and they have not had the means of education, nor would the children attend without they were under a master who had the authority over them, as the minister has made the attempt but failed.

It was left to Rev. Grey Cotes nearly ten years later to try again and in 1827 a small school was started in the chancel of the church.

A plan of the Rectory estate belonging to Rev. Samuel Smith in 1783, held by the Wiltshire and Swindon Record Office, shows it to include considerable arable and pasture land. Valuations of the living of Stanton St.

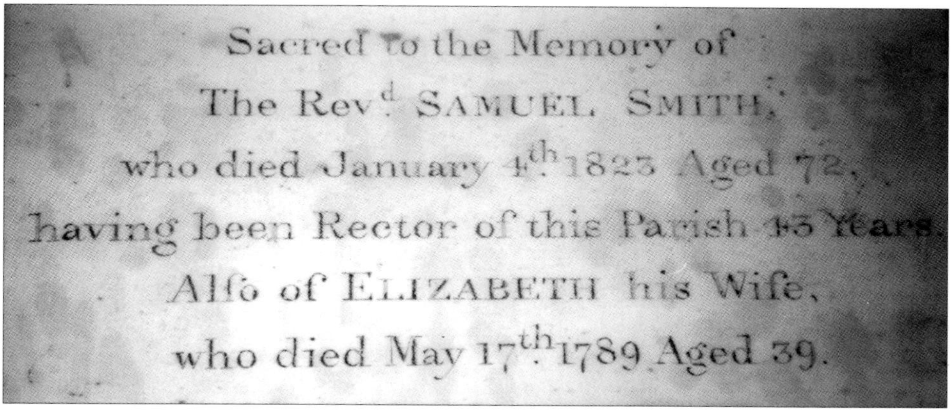

Memorial plaque to Rev. Samuel Smith (photograph by author)

Quintin – £8 in 1291, £10 6s in 1535 , £100 in 1650 and £ 312 circa 1830 – show the rectory to have been of slightly above average wealth and well endowed for a small parish.

The glebe land measured 118 acres in 1624, 135 acres in 1678 and about 150 acres in the early 18th century. From 1783 the Rector owned 409 acres of land plus a farm at Lower Stanton. Exchanges of land agreed in 1783 to redeem the Land Tax, reduced the glebe to 358 acres after 1804.

Samuel Smith remained Rector for 43 years, dying in 1823 aged 72. He was predeceased by his wife Elizabeth who died in 1789 at the relatively young age of 39. His successor on 14th March 1823 was Frederick Pleydell Bouverie (1785-1857), son of Jacob, the 2nd Earl Radnor.

For the next hundred years the Rectory was to undergo further major refurbishment and expansion.

4
Beneath the Weeping Willow

I could tell the characters of many of those who lie asleep in this churchyard as far as a man may judge but it would not be well. There are some little children, young bright holy youths and maidens – brave true holy men and women as well as some taken away in the midst of sin, and some without a moment's warning and hundreds whose very names are all long forgotten.

Reflections on St. Giles churchyard in the 19th century by Rev. Hon. Bertrand Bouverie

Much of the history of Stanton Court in the nineteenth century comes from the extensive archives of Canon J.E. Jackson, the notable Wiltshire antiquarian, and the personal diary of Rev. Hon Bertrand Bouverie, Rector of the parish between 1870 and 1880, (later known as Canon Bouverie). Both men were members of the Wiltshire Archaeological and Natural History Society, Canon Jackson being one of its founder members and first joint secretary.

Canon John Edward Jackson was born in Doncaster in 1805, one of eleven children. In 1823 he matriculated as a gentleman commoner at Brasenose College, Oxford, reading classics, and after graduating came to live in the West Country, initially as a companion to his elder brother who was a newly ordained curate at Farleigh Castle. It was his time at Farleigh that determined his career as both clergyman and antiquarian.

Jackson's first short book, written in 1842, was *The history of the parish of Grittleton,* which included a eulogy of Joseph Neeld, who bought the Grittleton estate in 1828, as a builder of model cottages and improver of roads. In 1845

Joseph Neeld appointed Jackson to the rectory of Leigh Delamere with Sevington, which after 1846 also included Norton. At that time Leigh Delamere and Sevington, with a population of about 113, and Norton, with a population of about 123, were isolated small rural parishes, their joint living about £380.

Joseph Neeld made huge improvements to the roads around Grittleton and its neighbouring estates and in Leigh Delamere rebuilt the Church, rectory, almshouse and manor farm as well as building the school at Sevington. Jackson became a lifelong friend of the Neeld family and on Joseph Neeld's death in 1856 he became joint executor of his estate.

Canon J.E. Jackson (from J Stratford, Catalogue of Jackson Collection, *1981)*

Jackson was a conscientious incumbent of his parishes and every Sunday would travel the eight miles between Leigh Delamere and Norton, walking, driving or riding, and he became well known within the diocese for being an eloquent speaker.

In 1852 he started the task of editing John Aubrey's *Wiltshire Topographical Collections*, a project which took ten years to finish, but which, on completion was described as the Wiltshire Archaeological and Natural History Society's *magnum opus*.

Jackson never married and once said that, 'he should always recommend any clergyman going to a quiet country parish to take a wife with him'. He was, however, a man who thrived in society and as an entertaining and humorous speaker could 'be relied upon to wake up any somnolent members of the audience'.

In 1863 Jackson became archivist to the 4th Marquis of Bath and became absorbed in the arrangement and publication of the Longleat collections. He died at Leigh Delamere in 1891. Upon his death he bequeathed fifteen volumes of manuscripts to the Wiltshire Archaeological and Natural History Society and fourteen volumes to the Society of Antiquaries of London.

The mid-nineteenth century was the great age of the foundation of county archaeological societies. Membership of the Wiltshire Archaeological and Natural History Society included other local luminaries such as William Henry Fox Talbot, squire of Lacock Abbey and inventor of photography. This was the Age of Enterprise and once again Wiltshire became associated with major achievements, such as Isambard Kingdom Brunel's Great Western Railway, which assumed great national importance. Canon Jackson himself kept a carriage and would often travel on the Great Western Railway from Chippenham to Bath, Oxford or London.

However, despite the technological advances of the age, medicine was practised more as an art than a science. It was at least one hundred years before the discovery of antibiotics and infant mortality was high. The Rev. Charles Grey Cotes and his wife Fanny Henrietta moved to Stanton Court in 1826 and were a much loved couple in the village. Sadly tragedy struck the family when four of their eight children died in infancy. A memorial in St. Giles Church commemorates the lives of Charles Robert, age 5, Shirley Grey, age 2 years 9 months, and Digby John, age 13 months, all of whom died within one month of each other of scarlet fever in 1845. A fourth child, George Washington, died as a baby in 1853. Of the four surviving children a son, Charles, married Hon. Lady Edith Bouverie, and a daughter, Maria, married Meredith Brown, both of whom were related to the Radnor family.

During his rectorship Rev. Grey Cotes added an East Wing to Stanton Court which at that time was known as Rectory House. The East wing incorporated offices at the back. He also had bay windows installed on the South side. The drawings overleaf show the South side of the house prior to Rev. Grey Cotes's incumbency and after his alterations.

The Grey Cotes devoted their lives and work to the people of the parish. In addition to their pastoral work Rev. Grey Cotes was a keen farmer and Fanny Grey Cotes took great pleasure in looking after the gardens at Stanton Court, which at that time attracted many admirers:

> Talking about the garden I have heard that in Rev. Cotes time the flower garden was the admiration of all beholders and that people would come miles to see it. It

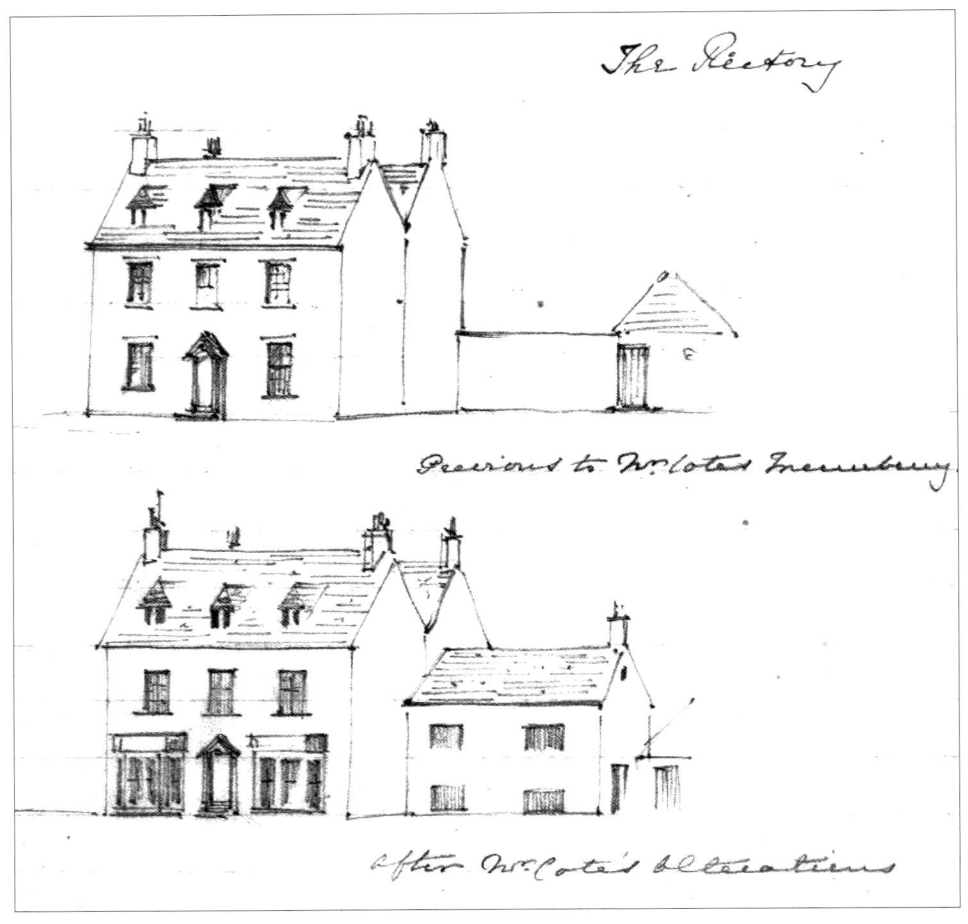

South side of the Rectory prior to Rev. Grey Cotes's incumbency and after his alterations (WSRO)

was laid out in Italian style and I have heard it compared to the richest Turkey carpet.

There were many occasions during Rev. Grey Cotes's rectorship when the gardens were enjoyed by all parishioners, such as the annual Harvest festival:

> The church was beautifully dressed with flowers on Thursday October 5th in celebration of the annual harvest thanksgiving. The service commenced at three o'clock with a crowded congregation, for this parish is so happily united that the large occupiers of land work together with the Rector in giving due honour to the Lord of the Harvest. The prayers were taken by the Rector, the Rev. Grey

> Cotes, the lesson read by the Rev. C.H.Awdry vicar of Seagry, the sermon preached by the Rev. J.J. Daniell incumbent of Langley Fitzhurse. Previously to the service the schoolchildren had been provided with dinner, after service there was a tea in the rectory gardens to which the whole body of parishioners was invited. Those who know the beauty of these gardens will understand that the scene presented on this occasion was pretty and interesting in the extreme.

Canon Jackson became a good friend of the Rev. and Mrs. Grey Cotes and would often dine with them at Stanton Court. He is also known to have preached in St. Giles Church, such as on the occasion which celebrated the completion of a major refurbishment of the church in 1851:

> The repairs of the larger part of the parish church of Stanton St Quintin having been completed, Thursday 18th was the day to celebrate its restoration. Stanton Church about 5 miles from Chippenham is well known for some points of great architectural beauty, particularly for its curious doorway and the three fine arches of the nave. These are rich examples of the Norman style and are in good preservation.
>
> The repair has been made at the expense of the patron Earl of Radnor, Viscount Folkestone and the Rev. C.G. Cotes ,Rector, aided by liberal contributions from the neighbourhood. It consists principally of the entire rebuilding of the South aisle and porch and the general restitution of all that was decayed in the lower and main body of the church.
>
> The interior has also been cleaned and put into order, the pews being replaced by open seats and the original oak roof being brought out by removal of a modern ceiling. The space between the tower (which stands between the nave and the chancel) has also been much improved by raising a low and heavy belfry floor and by re-opening two old and boldly displayed narrow light windows which were discovered blocked up by masonry in the thickness of the tower wall. The restoration of this curious and ancient church having been an object of much interest in the neighbourhood, a considerable number of the gentry and clergy with their families assembled on the day appointed at Rectory House. At the morning service the prayers were read by the Rector, assisted by the rural Dean, the Rev. Tuson, vicar of Minety after which a sermon from Haggai 1.9 was preached by the Rev. Thomas Legh Claythorn, a vicar of Kidderminster and Canon of Worcester.

In the afternoon the church was completely filled by a very numerous attendance of farmers and peasantry when a sermon from Hebrews XIII.8 was preached by the Rev. J.E.Jackson M.A., Rector of the adjoining parish of Leigh Delamere. Some very simple and impressive psalmody by twelve voices was kindly supplied from the villagers and schoolchildren of Rodbourne near Malmesbury.

For visitors of every degree there was hospitable entertainment provided in the rectory grounds and at the schoolhouse by Mr. and Mrs. Grey Cotes, and by Messrs. Miles and Hibbard the Churchwardens and Mr. Edmund Miles, at their respective houses. Among the company present were Viscount Wellesley of Draycote House, Mr. Esmeade High Sheriff, Mr. John Neeld MP, Mrs. Poulett Scrope , Mrs. Boldero etc

The collection after the service amounted to £50.

Fanny Grey Cotes died in 1865 and her death was much lamented in the parish. During her life she had been described as a nursing mother to the whole parish:

> she stretched out her hands to the poor, yea she reached forth her hands to the needy, she opened her mouth with wisdom and in her tongue was the law of kindness.

Sadly, after Fanny's death the gardens at Stanton Court became badly neglected.

The following year Charles Grey Cotes died, after forty years as Rector of the parish. His death notice described him as:

> an admirable farmer, he gave the peasantry large allotments, encouraged them to cultivate their land after the best methods and provided them with the best seeds and implements.

He was laid to rest alongside his wife and four children in St. Giles churchyard, beneath a weeping willow.

After Rev. Grey Cotes's death Stanton Court fell into a state of disrepair and it was left to the next incumbent, Canon F.J. Buckley, to make further repairs and refurbishments. Using £900 out of the dilapidation money received from the Grey Cotes family Canon Buckley had the whole South face of the house rebuilt, restoring the bay windows and installing a new roof in 1867. He also made the dramatic alteration of switching the entrance, which had been on the South side of the house, to the North. The original entrance hall on the South side was converted into a drawing room and what was the kitchen in Rev. Smith's time and a schoolroom in Rev. Cotes's time became the new entrance hall. Ironically further change in the 1950s would convert part of the entrance hall back to a kitchen. A driveway from the road was constructed on the north side which was said to be suitable for carts as well as carriages.

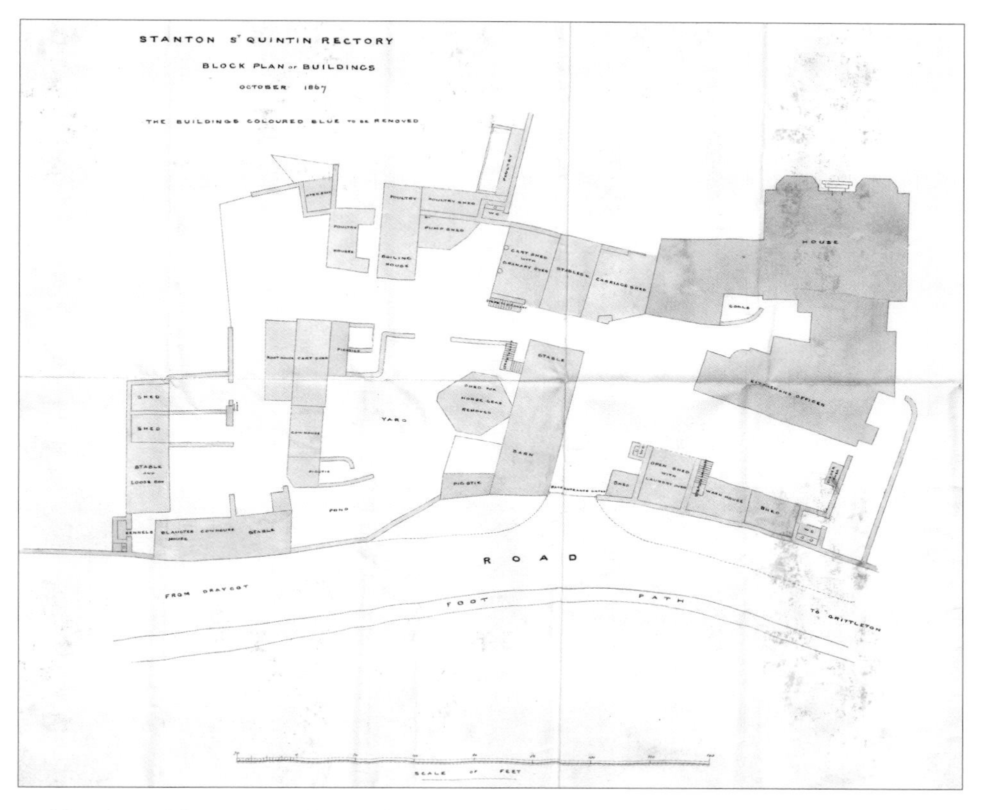

1867 Plan of the Rectory: the north wing was later completely remodelled (Bristol Record Office)

In 1870 Canon Buckley resigned as Rector to make way for his cousin Rev. Hon. Bertrand Bouverie. Stanton Court was about to undergo further major redesign.

5
'Patria Cara, Carior Libertas'

Goodness and mercy all my life
Shall surely follow me,
And in God's house for evermore
My dwelling place shall be.
Psalm 23

In 1870, two days before his twenty-fifth birthday, Rev. Hon. Bertrand Bouverie married Lady Constance Jane Nelson, and shortly afterwards the newly-weds took up residence at Stanton Rectory.

The Rev. Hon Bertrand Bouverie was the third son of Jacob, 4th Earl of Radnor. Like many of his generation, as the third son of a wealthy landowner he was destined for the Church, whilst it fell to the first son to inherit the family estate and the second son to enter the Army. As it happened, Bertrand Pleydell Bouverie had eight brothers and four sisters, two of whom died in infancy. His eldest brother William, the 5th Earl Radnor, was also MP for South Wiltshire between 1874 and 1885.

Bertrand Bouverie was born at Longford Castle, Wiltshire, the family seat of the Radnor family, in 1845, and educated at Harrow and Trinity College, Cambridge. At the age of 22 he was ordained as a curate by the Bishop of Worcester and spent two years in Halesowen before being presented to the rectory at Stanton St. Quintin by Lord Radnor. After ten years as Rector of Stanton St. Quintin the Bouveries moved to the parish of Pewsey, which was also in the living of the Radnor family, and Bertrand Bouverie became Rev. Hon. Canon Bouverie.

Longford Castle, Wilts. (reproduced by kind permission of Simmons Aerofilms Ltd)

Nelson boarding San Josef, by George Jones (© National Maritime Museum, London)

His wife, Lady Constance, was the daughter of the 3rd Earl Nelson, great nephew of Horatio Nelson. In Pewsey church the altar rails are formed out of part of the three-decker ship *San Josef* boarded by Horatio Nelson in 1797 in the Battle of Cape St. Vincent.

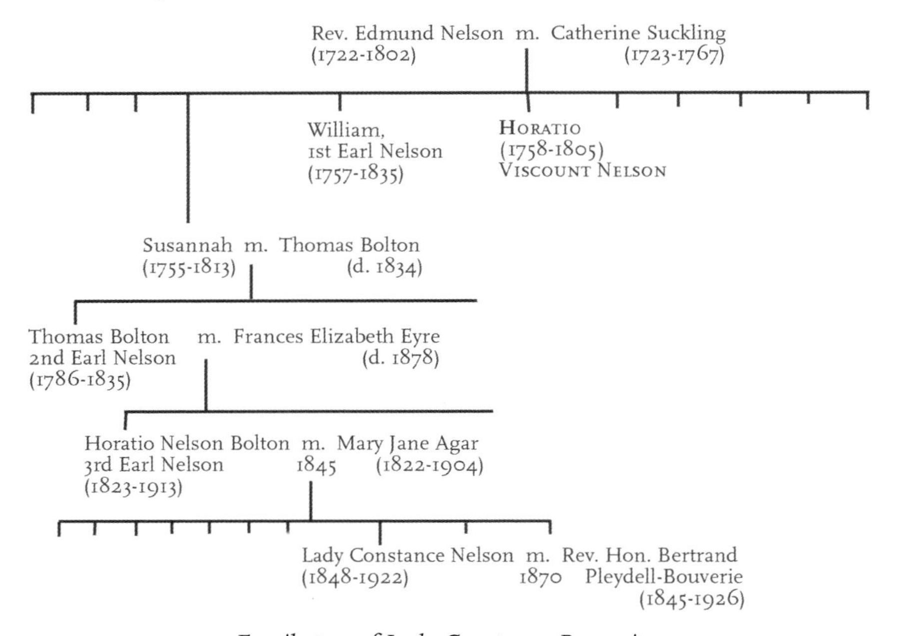

Family tree of Lady Constance Bouverie

When Bertrand Bouverie arrived at Stanton Rectory he recalled that, despite the repairs made by his predecessors, there was still scope for improvement:

> There were great improvements but the offices remained as they were, very bad. When I came to be Rector I found they were so bad, the drains and water supply so filthy that it was absolutely necessary to make great alterations therefore I proceeded to borrow on the living the sum of £1450 from Queen Anne's bounty, this in 1872.

Within two years of Bertrand Bouverie becoming Rector, Stanton Court underwent a dramatic redesign by Ewan Christian, the Ecclesiastical Commissioners' architect:

During the course of renovations three large cesspools were found under the house, the drains were described as being in a fearful state and the water

1872 pencil sketch of Rectory, from Rev. Hon. Bertrand Bouverie's diary (WSRO)

in the well completely poisoned. Rev. Bouverie recalls that in order to have a good supply of pure water all the rainwater off the roof of the house was collected into a large Bath stone tank and filtered, the drains were rearranged and a proper cesspool made in the kitchen garden which was now made on the east side of the farmyard instead of the west side of the house by the churchyard. New sheds were built, new entrance gates installed (now long since gone) and a new wall constructed round half the kitchen garden for wall fruit. Later parish records mention that when drainage operations were carried out, skeletons were found under stone slabs in the rectory garden.

Part of the refurbishment of the East Wing included the addition of an orangery, seen in the illustration. This was thought to have been dismantled at the beginning of the 20th century by Leslie Mann, who, together with his father and brother ran a family carpentry business, providing a service for the large estates nearby such as Badminton House, Grittleton House and Stanton Court. Once dismantled the glass from the orangery was used, much later, to build the greenhouse in the garden of the Old Post Office, where the Mann family lived for many years, and still stands today.

In addition to building the orangery, once again the South front of Stanton Court was rebuilt with two gables to replace three attic dormers. Another wing was built on the North side consisting of a kitchen, scullery, larder, dairy and

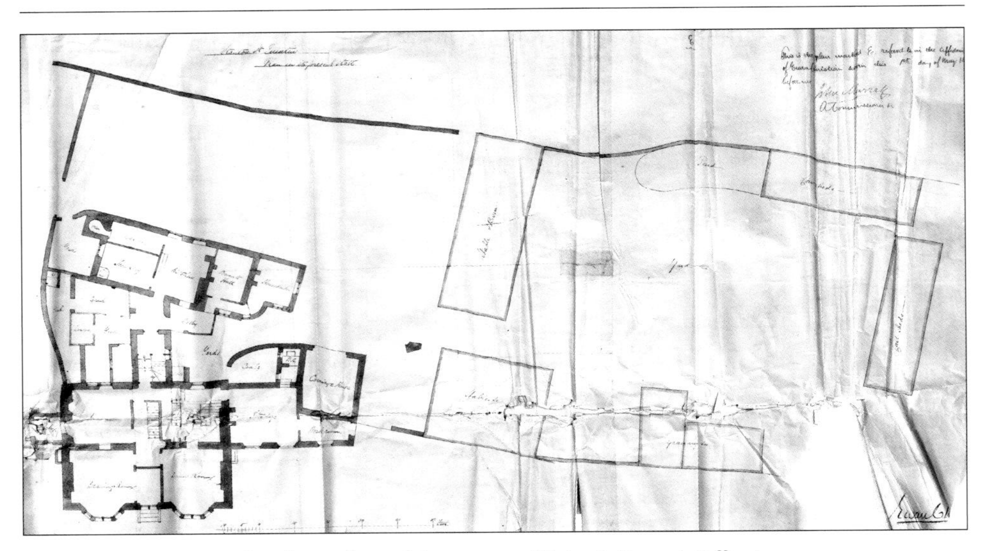

1871 floor plan of the rectory (Bristol Record Office)

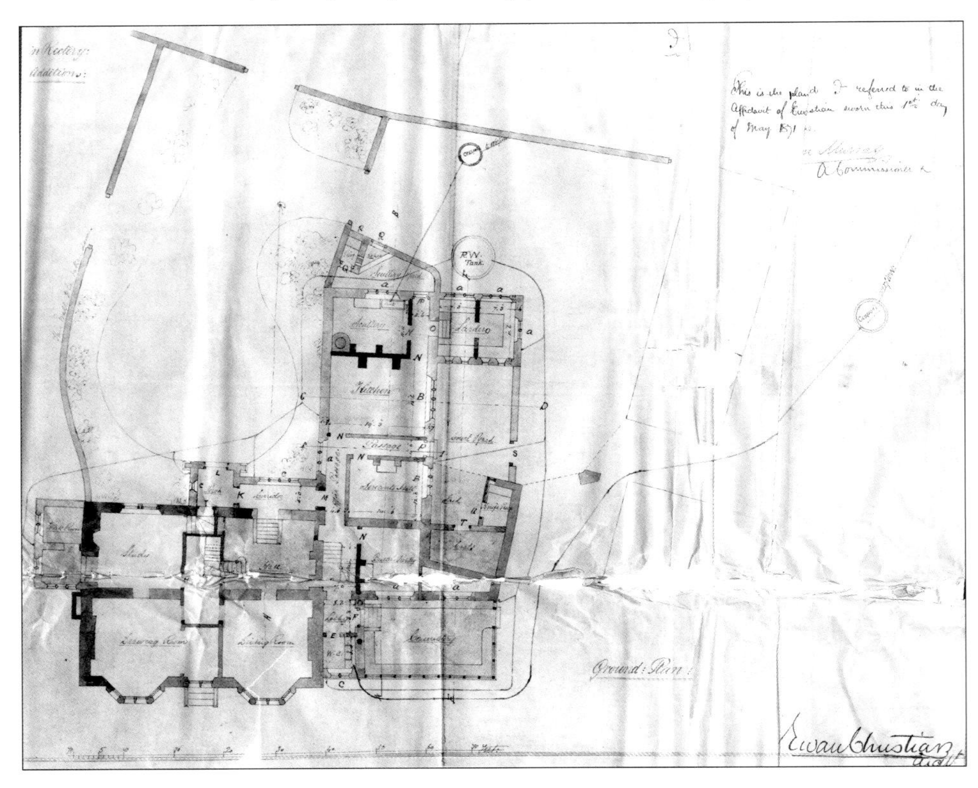

1872 following remodelling of north wing (Bristol Record Office)

servants' hall on the ground floor and three bedrooms and a housemaid's closet on the upper. What was originally Rev. Cotes's study in the East Wing became the pantry (renamed 'The Old Pantry' in 1992) and a low corridor connecting the North Wing to the central part of the house was now added together with a porch.

A striking feature of the interior of Stanton Court today is the oak panelling in the hall, dining room and main sitting room. Rev. Bouverie describes how he salvaged the wood from Purton church near Swindon, where once it had formed part of the old pulpit and reading desk, and he used it to panel the lower walls. An old stone fireplace which was placed in the entrance hall was presented to Rev. Bouverie by Sir John Neeld of Grittleton in 1875 and came from the Old Mansion House at Surrendell which was demolished in the 19th century. This fireplace no longer exists as it was removed in 1984 when the house was divided up and a new kitchen was derived from part of the entrance hall.

The handsome stone fireplace, from the Old Mansion house at Surrendell, which was presented to Rev. Bouverie by Sir John Neeld of Grittleton. Photographed in 1931. (Cannan collection).

Once the alterations to the house had been completed, Rev. Bouverie turned his attention to the garden, planting shrubs, making a lawn tennis court on the east side of the house and building a summerhouse on the west side, previously the site of the old kitchen garden, knocking down the wall between it and the churchyard and putting up an iron fence with arches for creepers. There is no doubt that during his relatively short incumbency of ten years, Rev. Bouverie made his mark on the parish, as did other members of the Radnor family.

The Radnor family, whose family motto is *Patria Cara, Carior Libertas,* ('my country is precious, but my freedom is more precious') were great benefactors in the village, starting a little school in 1848 and continuing their patronage until 1922. The Parish Census of 1871 denotes Emily Curtis, a 23-year-old schoolmistress, as residing at Stanton Rectory as a boarder. Stanton St. Quintin School started off as a Church of England School and remained so for over one hundred years until it changed to a County Primary School in 1955.

The Radnor family also owned Stanton Manor which had been sold to Sir Edward des Bouverie in 1718. It then passed to his brother Sir Jacob, 1st Viscount Folkestone and then to his son William who was created 1st Earl of Radnor in 1765. Ownership of Stanton Manor then passed from father to son through six generations of Radnors until 1909, when Lord Radnor sold it to Meredith Meredith Brown. His wife, Maria, was the daughter of Charles Grey Cotes, former rector of Stanton St. Quintin. Although the Manor was owned by the Radnor family, for most of this time it was a tenanted farmhouse.When Meredith Brown died in 1920 the Manor and its estate were divided up and sold.

The original Manor House which stood in John Aubrey's time was a large building with two main east–west ranges. In it were windows of the 13th, 14th and 15th centuries, derived from the time when the Manor belonged to the St. Quintin family. By marriage with an heiress of that family the Manor was transferred to Lord Dacres and thereafter it was given to the Abbey of Cirencester, as, according to Aubrey, 'it appears from the *Magna Britannia* that the Power family held it on lease from that convent for almost three hundred years.' Aubrey also states that the Manor was situated in a very extensive park surrounded by a high wall and the house had a moat, well stocked with fish, and an old fashioned gatehouse.

At the south-east corner of the house was an embattled two storey tower. According to Canon Jackson the ground floor of this tower was a small square room, apparently a prison, lighted only by loopholes, whilst the room above

Watercolour by John Buckler of Stanton Manor, 1808 (Wilts C.C., ex VCH collection)

had three oriel, or bay, windows on three different sides, in each of which were two seats or privies.

The tower was taken down circa 1810, the remainder of the house in 1856. A large stone farmhouse was built on its site, circa 1856-1857. North of the house was a circular 18th-century dovecote (still standing) and an early 19th-century barn which has since been converted into 21st-century residences.

The surviving dovecote (photograph by author)

It was during his incumbency in Stanton St. Quintin that Rev. Hon. Bertrand Bouverie began to develop his artistic skills which flourished when he became Rector of Pewsey for the following thirty years.

He became an accomplished sculptor, sculpting the stone pulpit, which was placed in St. Giles Church in 1893, and part of the tower pillars of St. Giles Church. In the parish church of St. John the Baptist in Pewsey is his carving, which he did from memory, of the *Pieta*, copied from the chapel of the Albergo de Pauvre in Genoa. He also carved an elaborate font cover, from wood.

He was also a keen water-colourist, sportsman, archaeologist and musician and took a close interest in community life.

Drawing (in WSRO) of St. Giles Church pulpit, sculpted by Canon Bouverie, above; and his carving of the Pieta*, church of St John the Baptist, Pewsey, below (photograph by author)*

Canon Bouverie was known for his wisdom as well as his sympathy and gentleness. He once told his congregation that he meant, with God as his helper, 'to try and follow in the steps of the Good Shepherd, and be a leader amongst them – not a driver, but a leader – one who should set an example and by kindly words and encouragement, as well as by warnings, try to lead those around him on the way to God.'

Canon Bouverie (Wilts C.C. P551)

When the Bouveries moved to Pewsey in 1880 the Canon once again became heavily involved in community life, becoming a magistrate, Chairman of the Parish Council, founding the St. John the Baptist's Communicants Society and chairing the Managers of the School Board.

There is no doubt that Canon Bouverie and his wife, Lady Constance, were well loved wherever they went. In later years Canon Bouverie often spent the winter months abroad due to failing health, and it is reported in Pewsey that on one occasion after his return from abroad after a severe illness the Rector and Lady Constance found themselves the centre of a great rejoicing, with the streets decorated with messages of welcome. A decorated carriage awaited them at the railway station from which they were drawn by hand through the streets to the rectory, amid cheering crowds.

In recognition of the Bouveries' contribution towards the community the old brewery premises in Pewsey were converted and renamed Bouverie Hall in 1899 and a housing development built in the 1960s in Stanton St. Quintin was named Bouverie Park. A new Bouverie Hall was opened in Pewsey to replace the old building in 1989.

Canon Bouverie died in November 1926 at the age of 82. His wife Lady Constance predeceased him and they are both buried at Pewsey Church, as well as Rev Frederick Pleydell Bouverie and his wife, who were also incumbents at Stanton St Quintin in the early 19th century.

Incumbency of the Parish of St. Giles 1780-1923.

	Patron	*Rector*
1780	Jacob, 2nd Earl of Radnor	Samuel Smith
1823	Jacob, 2nd Earl of Radnor	Frederick Pleydell Bouverie
1826	Jacob, 2nd Earl of Radnor	Charles Grey Cotes
1867	Jacob, 3rd Earl of Radnor	Canon F.J.Buckley
1870	Jacob, 4th Earl of Radnor	Hon. Bertrand Bouverie
1880	Jacob, 4th Earl of Radnor	Canon F.J. Buckley (for second turn)
1905	Jacob, 6th Earl of Radnor	H. Dillon Trenchard
1907	Jacob, 6th Earl of Radnor	Geoffrey Henslow
1911	Meredith Brown	Frederick Wm. Stephens Price
1923	The Bishop of Bristol	Gordon Tidy

The incumbent in 1907 was the Rev. Geoffrey Henslow who lived at Stanton Rectory for four years. In 1911 he was given dispensation by the bishop of Bristol to move to another parish and the contents of Stanton Rectory were put up for sale by auction.

The last incumbent, Rev. Frederick Price, arrived in 1911, but after 12 years upkeep of Stanton Rectory was becoming too much of an encumbrance for the Diocese and it was time to move on.

THE RECTORY,
STANTON ST. QUINTIN,
CHIPPENHAM, WILTS.

CATALOGUE
OF A GREAT ASSEMBLAGE OF
Antique Furniture,
THE MODERN
Furnish of the Rectory,
Together with the Widely-Renowned
ROSARY,
AND
OUT-DOOR EFFECTS,
WHICH

HERBERT PARRY & FERRIS

Have received instructions from the Rev. T. G. W. Henslow, M.A.,
to Sell by Auction upon the Premises,

On Tuesday, 7th March, 1911,
AND 3 FOLLOWING DAYS,
Commencing at 11 o'clock a.m., prompt each day.

Valuing and Estate Offices,
39, Market Place, Chippenham,
Calne and Devizes.

Telephone 33 Chippenham Telegrams "HERBERT PARRY."

1911 Auction catalogue, Stanton St Quintin Rectory (E. Gibb)

6
The Cocktail Years

As sunlight streamed through the mullion windows of Stanton Court, the sound of laughter could be heard from the garden below. A blonde mop of hair poked out from the first floor schoolroom window and turning excitedly to Miss Fry, her governess, the little girl proclaimed
'Mama is entertaining the Princess for lunch today!'

In 1924 the Bishop of Bristol sold Stanton Rectory to Hon. Mrs. Cyril Ward, and the rectory was renamed Stanton Court. As a private residence for the gentry, Stanton Court was about to enter one of the most colourful phases in its history attracting royalty, the literati and the gliterati.

The Hon. Mrs Cyril Ward was a Dutch lady, known as Baroness Irene de Brienen, before her marriage to Capt. Hon. Cyril Augustus Ward, son of the 1st Earl of Dudley, in 1904. She is not to be confused with Freda Dudley Ward, erstwhile mistress of the Duke of Windsor, who married the nephew of the 1st Earl of Dudley. Nonetheless both ladies had a penchant for property development and interior design!

The Hon. Mrs. Cyril Ward purchased Stanton Court for £3,150 and she immediately found it necessary to spend another £3,500 on installing a drainage system, adding a West Wing of four rooms in 1926 and generally modernising the house which in 1922 had been described by its ecclesiastical incumbent as being, 'much too large, a very cold house with no modern conveniences', and that it was 'impossible to get servants to reside there'. It is quite possible that Mrs. Ward lived at Stanton Court for only a very short time, preferring instead to renovate it and lease it, although this is conjecture. For a short while she herself was a tenant at Norton Manor and after her divorce she married Vice Admiral Hon. Arthur Strutt and moved to Shipton Moyne.

Meanwhile parish records state that:

> after much discussion and indecision as to the site, water was found for a new rectory alongside the road between the two villages and to the south of the stream the road crosses. Owing to the indecisions of the incumbent and the Diocesan architect the building of the new rectory was not begun and the Rector continued to live in lodgings in Hullavington.

A new stone rectory house in vernacular style was finally completed in 1928 on the road between Upper and Lower Stanton and this house was sold in 1975 to Mr. and Mrs.L.Plummer whilst the rectory moved to a new house in Rectory Close within Upper Stanton

Capt. and Mrs. Astley Cannan and their two children, Helen and John, were the next family to occupy Stanton Court possibly initially as tenants, although it is known that Capt. Cannan of the 5th Lancers bought the Court in 1927.

Capt. and Mrs. Astley Cannan (reproduced by kind permission of the Cannan family)

Photographs of the Court at that time show a grand estate with sweeping manicured lawns, tennis courts and several outbuildings which were used as stables and garages. The yew avenue to the south of the house was then in its infancy and the adjacent little wood, which thrives eighty years later, not yet in existence. Instead the view from the house encompassed miles of rolling pasture punctuated only by a majestic oak, imposing cast iron gates and a stone ha-ha, all of which exist today although the oak tree has acquired considerably more hollows, the gates more moss and the ha-ha is sadly overgrown.

Stanton Court grounds in 1931 (Cannan collection)

Upkeep of such a grand estate required a large household of staff. Helen Cannan recalls that the staff comprised a governess, butler, footman, three housemaids, a chef, a cook, three other kitchen staff, three gardeners, two grooms and a chauffeur.

Capt. Cannan's chauffeur was Bernard Hazel. He had previously worked for the Duke of Beaufort at Badminton and his family lived in Stanton St.Quintin, in one of the houses opposite Manor Farm. His daughter, Betty Boast, remembers attending Stanton St. Quintin School with Bernard Anstee,

Exterior view of Stanton Court in 1931 (Cannan collection)

which at that time consisted of a single Victorian classroom. She also recalls Mrs. Thomas, the Welsh schoolmistress, who lived at St. Edith's across the Malmesbury Road, and who ruled with a rod of iron making the school children sing 'Bread of Heaven' every morning.

Bernard Hazel, Betty's father, would drive Capt. Cannan to London, along the A4, on a regular basis and no sooner had he arrived back in Stanton than a message would be received by phone *('Kington Langley 22')* for him to turn around again immediately and collect Capt. Cannan for the return journey. The journey would be made in either the Captain's Alfa Romeo or Chrysler, although the Cannan children clearly recall enjoying rides in the dickie seat of their father's Vauxhall. The cars were garaged on the site now occupied by the Coach House, and the adjoining stables were where the Cannans kept their five horses and two ponies , on a site which was later converted to Stables Cottage.

Hazel, as he was known by the Cannans, was a most genial man and, as Helen Cannan recalls, had a kindly face. He would often take the children, dressed in all their finery, out to afternoon tea in their pony and trap. On one notable occasion the pony bolted and the trap ended up in a nearby pond alongside a couple of bedraggled children.

Bernard Hazel eventually left Capt. Cannan's employment when he bought and settled at the Bell Inn in Yatton Keynell with his family and he is fondly remembered there not least because he kept a pet fox which was partial to supping the occasional half-pint of ale.

His wife Nell Hazel had been seamstress to Mrs. Marjorie Cannan, who was a most gracious and elegant lady, as photographs of her riding side saddle with the Beaufort hunt bear witness. The Cannans would ride out with the Beaufort Hunt two or three times per week and John Cannan, then aged about four years old, soon mastered this skill.

John Cannan with his parents, Beaufort Hunt (Cannan collection)

John Cannan was educated at boarding school, attending Burton Grange, Rugby then Eton and subsequently attending Sandhurst, whilst Helen, his sister, like most well-to-do girls of her generation, was educated at home, by Miss Fry. The schoolroom can be identified quite clearly on old photographs of the house by the globe which sat in the window of the first floor room in the

Mrs. Marjorie Cannan (Cannan collection)

His Grace 10th Duke of Beaufort, to the left of the picture, with Capt. Cannan, centre, and the Beaufort Hunt (Cannan collection)

East Wing which is now the Old Pantry. A home education was by no means inferior however and credit is due, in part, to Miss Fry for the fact that Helen subsequently became multilingual, a qualification which stood her in good stead later on in life as the wife of a senior diplomat.

The young children lived in the North Wing of Stanton Court, which comprised the kitchens on the ground floor and bedrooms on the 1st floor, whilst the East Wing at that time comprised the pantry and stores on the ground floor and schoolroom on the 1st floor. Some of the servants occupied the top floor of Stanton Court whilst others lived locally. Every afternoon the children would be summoned to join their parents at four o'clock and they would descend via the back staircase to the drawing room to join their mother around the grand piano.

Music and the arts featured strongly in life at the Court in those days and the Cannans were a sociable couple. The 10th Duke of Beaufort was a regular guest as were certain members of the Royal family, in particular Princess Marie Louise.

Princess Marie Louise was the granddaughter of Queen Victoria. She was born at Cumberland Lodge, Windsor in 1872, the fourth child of Princess

Princess Marie Louise (right), and with Prince Aribert of Anhalt (left)
(The Royal Collection, © Her Majesty Queen Elizabeth II)

Helena and Prince Christian Schleswig-Holstein. At the age of nineteen she married Prince Aribert of Anhalt but sadly the marriage was annulled by her father-in-law nine years later. This may have turned out to be a blessing in disguise for the young princess, who had an adventurous spirit and probably found the restrictive environment of court life in a small German principality too stifling. Once her marriage was over, Louie, as she was known within the Royal Family, became a free spirit travelling the world and writing several books. She was undoubtedly a modern princess, whom in many respects was ahead of her time. The Princess valued her many friendships and although she enjoyed a privileged lifestyle she worked hard for many charitable causes. She frequently stayed at Chavenage House in Gloucestershire and was a visitor to many West Country estates, including Stanton Court, some of which she wrote about in her book *My Memories of Six Reigns*. In this book she recounts in some detail the etiquette which would attend such occasions. Looking at photographs of Stanton Court at this time it is easy to be transported back to an era of silver service at tea, summoning the maid via the service bell and dressing for dinner.

Interior of Stanton Court, 1931, above and following pages. (all Cannan collection)

The Drinking Room (above); the Dining Room in the West Wing (below), both 1931

The Drinking Room (above); the Drawing Room looking west (below), both 1931

The Drawing Room looking east, 1931

The service bell (although now non functioning!) still exists in the main drawing room; and the room which, at the time of writing, is the dining room in Stanton Court was known in the 1930s as the drinking room. It was here that the gentlemen of the house would meet before dinner, and retire post-prandially to enjoy their port, brandy and cigars.

The dining room in those days was in the West Wing and a service corridor was used to bring food here from the kitchen in the North Wing. It is interesting also to note that there is a ground floor room in the North Wing which abuts eastwards which was used as the cold room (and indeed subsequent occupants have stated that it is notoriously difficult to keep this room warm in winter!). It also transpires that the secret passageway in the cellar of Stanton Court, which comes to a dead end on the north side of the building, once led to an underground ice house, which was a necessity in a large household, before the days of electricity. The ice house was situated under where our garage now stands.

Fans of Lord Emsworth, Bertie Wooster and his butler Jeeves may be forgiven, when studying photos of Stanton Court in the Thirties, for thinking that these characters would not look out of place in this environment. Consider the following extract from *Summer Lightning* by P.G. Wodehouse, written in 1929:

> . . . there sounded through the mellow, drowsy stillness a drowsy, mellow chiming. It was the clock over the stables striking five. Simultaneously, a small but noteworthy procession filed out of the house and made its way across the sunbathed lawn to where the big cedar tree cast a grateful shade. It was headed by James, a footman, bearing a laden tray. Following him came Thomas, another footman, with a gate-leg table. The rear was brought up by Beach (the butler), who carried nothing but merely lent a tone.

The setting here was Blandings Castle, the imaginary quintessentially English manor house which was loosely based on the Wodehouse family home near Bridgnorth in Shropshire. However the author also conceded in an interview with the *Observer* in 1971 that 'Blandings was a sort of mixture of places I remembered'.

The Study in the West Wing, 1931 (Cannan collection)

It may delight the reader to know, therefore, that P.G. Wodehouse was another celebrated guest to have spent time at Stanton Court and it is perfectly possible that Sir Pelham Grenville Wodehouse (known as 'Plum') garnered material for his comic novels from his stay here. Certainly he was known to have occupied the study which today forms the west-facing ground floor room of the West Wing, and he was a great friend of the family. Indeed his step-daughter Leonora Cazalet (wife of Peter Cazalet the Queen Mother's racehorse trainer) was godmother to Helen Cannan.

P.G. Wodehouse photographed in 1928 (Hulton Getty)

Betty Boast clearly remembers the fun to be had every year when Capt. and Mrs. Cannan would invite all the village children to tea in the gardens of Stanton Court to celebrate Empire Day on May 24th. John Cannan fondly remembers Chips, the Sealyham terrier, featured in some of the photographs, who would frequently wander into St. Giles Church during a service and join in by whining when the choir started singing, and Countess Badeni recalls going for picnics as a child in Stanton Park with the Cannan children and their respective nannies.

The Depression of the 1930s was to wreak great sorrow on many families but despite the gloom there are many happy memories of this bygone age.

7
Daisy Chains and Tiaras

Maidens, if a maid you meet
Always free from pout and pet,
Ready smile and temper sweet,
Greet my little Margaret.
And if loved by all she be
Rightly, not a pampered pet,
Easily you then may see
'Tis my little Margaret.

An Acrostic by Lewis Carroll.

In 1931 Lady Margaret Spicer purchased Stanton Court from Capt. Cannan. She had moved from the family estate at Spye Park near Bromham, home to the Spicer family since 1863, following the death of her husband, Capt. John Spicer, and the marriage of her son Capt Frank Spicer to Lady Avice Sackville-West.

Despite a life of great privilege, Lady Margaret (who, as the daughter of an earl, always used this style of address in preference to Lady Spicer) lived a life touched by tragedy but shaped by munificence to others. The daughter of the 12th Earl of Westmoreland, she was born Lady Margaret Mary Fane at Apethorpe Hall, Northamptonshire in 1870; however within her close family she was always known as Daisy. A childhood portrait of her with her younger brother Lord Burghersh shows a little girl who would not look out of place on the pages of *Through the Looking Glass,* with long blonde hair, swept back in an Alice band. A later portrait by John Singer Sargeant depicts her gradual transformation into a handsome elegant woman with regal aquiline features.

At the age of 18 she married Capt. John Edmund Philip Spicer, who was twenty years her senior. They had been introduced to each other at Badminton House and together they enjoyed a happy marriage of forty years, during which time Lady Margaret had seven children. Family life, and the welfare of her children, were paramount to Lady Margaret.

Lady Margaret and Lady Grace Fane (John Spicer)

Her only daughter Joan worked tirelessly as a Voluntary Aid Detachment nurse at Bowood during the First World War, but tragically became a victim of the Spanish flu pandemic and died in 1919 at the age of 23. Another child, John, had died of appendicitis in 1906 at the age of 15, and in 1928 the eldest of her five surviving sons, Capt. Anthony Spicer, was killed in a tragic accident at Spye Park, within one year of inheriting the family estate when, during fierce gales, he was crushed to death by a falling tree. (A similar tragedy occurred the same year in Stanton St. Quintin during a great storm, when a young schoolgirl, Kitty Holder, was also killed by a falling tree).

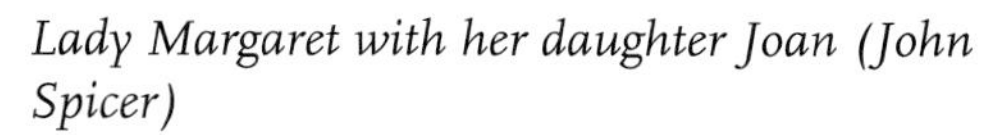

Lady Margaret with her daughter Joan (John Spicer)

Lady Margaret was a vivacious lady with a keen sense of fun. She loved music and the arts and excelled at working tapestries and painting watercolours. In the early days of her marriage she would often take a tandem tricycle ride into Bath with her husband, for lunch at the Pump Room. On other occasions, prior to a game of tennis, she would remove her rather large weighty diamond engagement ring from her hand and place it on the yew hedge before scattering gardeners in all directions looking for it when she proclaimed she couldn't find it.

Capt. J. E. Spicer and Lady Margaret at a point-to-point in the Twenties (Spicer collection)

The Fane – Spicer family were well connected, and as well as counting the Marquis of Lansdowne at Bowood , and the Duke and Duchess of Beaufort at Badminton, amongst their friends, they frequently mixed in royal circles. Lady Margaret's brother Lord Burghersh was part of the social set which included Edward, Prince of Wales (later to become the Duke of Windsor) and Freda Dudley Ward. Many years later Lady Avice Spicer forged a lifelong friendship with Her Majesty Queen Elizabeth, the Queen Mother, who was an annual guest at Spye Park between 1953 and 1968 and who occasionally visited Stanton St. Quintin.

However it is Her Majesty Queen Mary whose name draws the greatest association with Stanton Court. Lady Margaret was, for many years, a friend of Her Majesty Queen Mary. In the 1920s and 30s the Queen was a frequent visitor to the Cotswolds staying at Badminton House, and attending Malmesbury Abbey; and she was often seen around the locality, visiting Stanton Court and later, during the Second World War, visiting Lady Margaret at Queenwood Lodge, Bowood.

Her Majesty Queen Mary with New Zealand lumberjacks who were billeted at Grittleton House, 1945 (© Annette and Mike Wilson)

When Lady Margaret moved to Stanton Court in 1931 she lived there with her youngest son Edmund, who later married Barbara Neeld. For the next ten years Stanton Court became the nucleus for Spicer family gatherings, whether at Christmas or at ceremonies such as christenings. On taking up residence in the village, Lady Margaret quickly earned the respect of the villagers and she is still remembered fondly by many, in particular Mrs. Elizabeth Anstee, whose mother-in-law Rose was a laundress for several of the large houses in the area.

In the 1930s, during the height of the Depression, Lady Margaret formed the Personal Service League together with Countess June Badeni's mother Mrs. Hilda Wilson. This was a charitable organisation to help families who had fallen on hard times. She was also instrumental in starting the tradition of the annual village fête in the gardens of Stanton Court, a tradition which has continued over many years, and which during the Depression raised money for the families of Welsh miners.

Lady Margaret's village fêtes in the gardens of Stanton Court are legendary. In 1937 a fête was held at the Court to celebrate the Coronation of

Rose and William Anstee in 1914 (Elizabeth and Bernard Anstee)

George VI and this raised £115 which was spent on dorsal and riddal curtains. At the same time Lady Margaret and Mr. and Mrs. Basil Hankey of Stanton Manor donated two altar frontals to St. Giles Church.

Lady Margaret also took an active interest in school affairs. The school records of November 1934 mention a special visit to the school by Lady Margaret, who had purchased musical instruments for the school percussion band. The school went on to enter many local music festivals over the years. The village school also enjoyed a long association with Mr. and Mrs. Hankey.

Basil and Maud Hankey came to Stanton St. Quintin in 1920 when they bought the Manor plus its estate. They took a great interest in the community and were generous benefactors to the school and church. Basil Hankey was responsible for continuing the Parish notes which had been begun by Rev. Bouverie. Of particular historical interest he noted that in 1932 a public electricity supply was introduced to the village.

Three years later, in 1935, the Air Ministry purchased 168 acres of land at Bell Farm, west of the Chippenham–Malmesbury road, from Mr. F. Huntley, and commenced construction of an RAF aerodrome, to which a further 45 acres were added later. In 1937 the aerodrome opened and 550 servicemen were added to the population of the Parish. In 1938 a new church hall was built on land given by Mr. Tanner the farmer, between Upper and Lower Stanton at a total cost of £818.

Stanton Court continued to evolve as a magnet for social gatherings of family and friends, thanks to Lady Margaret's warmth and the high regard in which she was held as a matriarch.

Meanwhile the storm clouds were gathering over Europe.

8

Damp Greatcoats, Serge Blankets and Stewed Tea

A gentle breeze filtered through the yew trees lifting the poppy petals that lay on eleven new graves in St. Giles churchyard. An issue bicycle came into view at the end of the street, as its rider, a young woman with greatcoat flapping, pedalled furiously past the Post Office before turning abruptly left into the driveway of Stanton Court.

The year was 1942 and Stanton Court was now a temporary home for 100 servicewomen of the Womens Auxiliary Air Force. Two years earlier Lady Margaret Spicer had temporarily moved to Queenwood Lodge on the Bowood Estate and had loaned Stanton Court to the Royal Air Force as part of the war effort. Very soon afterwards scores of women were drafted in, as volunteers or conscripts, to work at nearby RAF Hullavington, which by 1942 had become the Empire Central Flying School.

One of these women was Aircraft Woman 2nd class 2146391, who at the age of 21 decided to leave the cosy environs of Washington D.C, and cross the Atlantic to join up. Her name was Mary Lee Settle and she went on to become a best selling novelist in the USA. Her book *All the Brave Promises* recounts her experience as a WAAF and includes reminiscences of her time at Stanton Court.

Ms. Settle worked as a radio operator, sitting in the flying control tower, guiding in the Airspeed Oxfords on their night flying exercises.

RAF Hullavington had opened in 1937 and was initially built as a flying training school; however it soon expanded to include an Aircraft Storage Unit, which by 1945 had over 1,000 aircraft in storage.

The aerodrome was originally home to no.9 Flying Training School, equipped with the single engine bi-plane, the Hawker Hart, but by spring 1939 twin engine Avro Anson trainers had been added to the fleet, followed by Airspeed Oxfords, and the unit was redesignated as no.9 Service Flying Training School.

With the declaration of war in Sept 1939 no evacuees were allocated to the parish, on account of the proximity of the aerodrome, and there were several occasions when the parish was subjected to enemy fire.

The cover of All the Brave Promises *by Mary Lee Settle*

Despite this it was business as usual at the village school. Every child was provided with a gas mask and took part in a weekly gas mask drill. In the event of an air raid the school children were evacuated across the road to take shelter in the cellar at Stanton Court.

However, as Ruby Jeffrey, a wartime pupil, explains, the warnings were not always given by conventional siren:

> Living in a very small village we did not have a siren to sound an air raid warning but at RAF Hullavington, which we could see from our playground, there was a red brick water tower and on top of the tower was a flagpole. If there was a raid likely – German aircraft 15 miles away – the flag was raised to half mast, and if they were in our locality the flag went to the top of the pole. Every day one of the more senior pupils would be detailed to go into the playground every fifteen minutes and check the flagpole. If the flag was at half mast we had to evacuate the school and go to our shelter. The shelter was a room across the road at

Stanton Court. It had no windows and was fairly well protected by the main building. At the time it seemed preferable to sit in the shelter waiting for bombs than to be in our classroom with Mrs. Thomas. She was a real dragon.

By 1940 air raid warnings were a regular occurrence. Anti-aircraft defensive armament was installed on the airfield, and trenches, gun pits and concrete pillboxes were constructed.

Some of the Ansons and Audaxes were converted to carry bombs for possible deployment as an anti-invasion force and many of the WAAFs were tasked to service the aeroplanes.

WAAF flight mechanics carrying out an inspection of an Oxford training aircraft (photograph courtesy of the Imperial War Museum, London CH10667)

One night in Summer 1940 Luftwaffe raiders attacked the airfield, dropping five bombs, but luckily without causing any damage. However as night flying training was constantly interrupted by the threat of enemy air raids, aircraft would be flown over to Babdown Airfield near Tetbury for night training exercises, returning in the early hours of the morning, and this continued until the end of the war.

On 14th August 1940 a local air defence patrol was just returning to the airfield when it was raided by Heinkel He IIIs. The German aircraft dropped sixteen bombs on the station, killing four airmen in a hangar and

Stanton war graves (author)

wounding another ten. A fuel bowser was hit and exploded, badly damaging several Harts and two Hurricanes and in another raid a high explosive bomb fell on Mr. Jones's farm at Lower Stanton and wrecked it. One of the servicemen who died in this air raid is buried in St. Giles Churchyard, alongside ten of his RAF colleagues, half of whom were pilots under training, and who were also killed during the Second World War.

The Winter of 1940 brought severe weather conditions. Stanton Court, stripped of its fine furnishings, was bleak but certainly not soulless. WAAFs returning from evening shift on the base would sit with their mugs of stewed tea, huddled around Bertrand Bouverie's fireplace in the large entrance hall before wending their way upstairs via the large oak staircase to their dormitories. Then, struggling to keep warm in their cots, weighted down by their brown serge blankets, they would talk long into the night, their voices misting the air. For some the scene may have parodied boarding school were it not for the heavy blackout curtains, the closed wooden shutters and the roar of overhead planes.

In the summer the garden was a pleasant sanctuary for many of the girls when off duty. Here they could relax in the shade of the magnolia tree, reading their letters and sharing stories from home.

John Cannan recalls a time towards the end of the War when curiosity got the better of him on a return trip to the village where he grew up. He was peering over the wall of the churchyard into Stanton Court and could see that the French window was open, so climbing over the wall into the garden he decided to take a closer look at the house which for him held precious childhood memories.

It was only when he was met by squeals of laughter and surprise and came face to face with several WAAFs in various states of undress that he turned tail and made a quick exit.

In 1941 two more air raids were made on RAF Hullavington. In February a Heinkel He III bombed and strafed the airfield damaging several aircraft but thankfully not taking any human casualties, and later on in the year a German aircraft was flying in close proximity to the airfield when it was detected by a RAF night fighter. The German pilot jettisoned his bomb cargo as part of his attempts to escape and once again damage was incurred to aircraft.

By 1942 RAF Hullavington became home to the Empire Central Flying School, which moved from Upavon, and its courses attracted student pilots from all over the world, including Canada, Australia, Poland, the USA, New Zealand and South Africa.

The School was to produce many distinguished and highly accomplished flying instructors who made a significant impact on the flying training programmes of the Allied Nations.

After the War Count Jan Badeni of the Polish Air Force served as a pilot to trainee navigators at RAF Hullavington between 1949 and 1951. In 1956 he married June Wilson of Norton Manor, and in 1978 became High Sheriff of Wiltshire.

Whilst RAF Hullavington attracted trainees from all over the Empire, many villagers joined the Armed Forces and saw active service abroad. Frank Randall, originally from Carlisle, trained with the Artillery Regiment as an anti-tank gunner at Catterick, and saw active service in France before returning to England and meeting Hannah Eliza Couzens. Hannah, or 'Nan' as she was known to all her family, grew up in Lower Stanton, went to the Village School and was in service at Stanton Court in the Thirties to the Cannan family. She and Frank were married by Canon Cornwall at St. Giles Church on Christmas Eve 1942. Towards the end of the War Nan worked as a civilian cook to no.9 Maintenance Unit, RAF Hullavington and Frank went on to work both at

Stanton Manor as a gardener to Mr Basil Hankey and in a civilian role at the airfield.

Another villager, Bernard Anstee, who spent most of his life in Stanton St. Quintin, joined the Army in 1933 and saw active service with the Wiltshire Regiment until 1946.

Tragically Basil and Maud Hankey lost both their sons in the War. Major Wyndham Hankey of the Wiltshire Regiment was killed in Normandy in 1944 and was buried in Calvados, and the following year Major Peter Hankey, of the Royal Horse Artillery was also killed on active service. Their father Basil died in 1948 and was buried alongside Peter in St. Giles Churchyard. Inside St. Giles Church there is a memorial to both sons, which was placed there by Mrs. Maud Hankey in 1948.

The wedding of Frank Randall and Hannah Couzens at St. Giles Church, 1942 (Frank Randall)

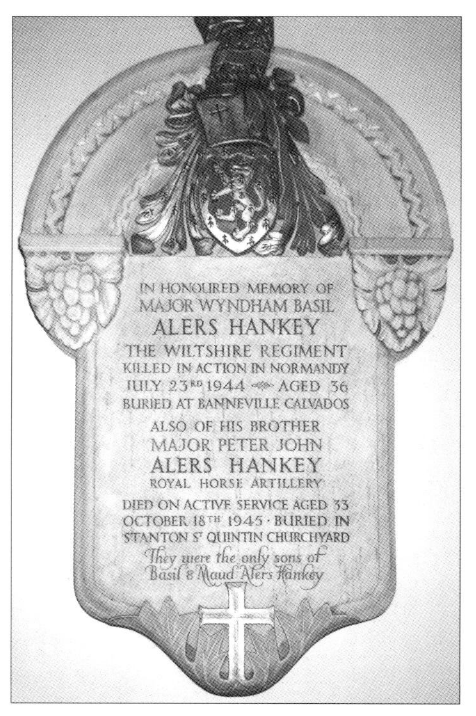

Memorial to the sons of Basil and Maud Hankey, St. Giles Church (author)

After July 1942 no enemy raids occurred within the parish and the WAAFs continued in their wide variety of roles as drivers, navigators, cooks and mechanics. Lifelong friendships were struck and the occasional romance blossomed. The villagers continued to

Two WAAF cooks at work at an RAF aerodrome (photograph courtesy of the Imperial War Museum, London CH6747)

be outnumbered by service personnel, and MT vehicles were a frequent sight in the street.

Every night an Admin. Corporal, huddled in a greatcoat, would sit in the gloom of the panelled drawing room of Stanton Court, checking in the WAAFs, the shadows heightened by the lack of furniture save a small table and folding chair. Outside the mullion windows the weeds grew up through the terraced paving and the grass remained uncut and untended whilst the roses grew wild.

Upstairs, caps with black shining peaks, and Air Force blue tunics and stockings, hung neatly over the sides of the cots whilst the smell of damp wool mingled with the unmistakeable smell of brass polish.

The WAAFs eventually vacated Stanton Court at the end of the War although many service personnel remained in the village. Active flying ceased at

Interior of Stanton Court, 1951, above and right (Gillian Howard)

the base in 1965 and the last RAF unit to be based at Hullavington was no. 4626 Aeromedical Evacuation Squadron , Royal Auxiliary Air Force. Although the base is currently home to no.9 Supply Regiment, Royal Logistics Corp, who moved there in 1993, one of the residential areas on the base is named Anson Place in recognition of the link with its past as a flying training school.

Lady Margaret moved back to Stanton Court after the War and spent her latter years being looked after by her daughter-in-law, Barbara (née Neeld, who had married Lady Margaret's son Edmund). Barbara became known locally, with affection, as 'Mrs. Eddie'. Lady Margaret died in 1949 and was buried in the family graveyard at Chittoe, near Spye Park.

Parish notes record that in 1949 Rev. Francois de Chaumont applied for a Parish Council and this was granted. The Rector was elected Chairman and the other elected councillors included Mr. R. Burridge, Mr. Albert Smith, Mr. Henry Tanner and Mr. Cecil Smith. Over fifty years later the author, Fiona Baskett, was privileged to serve three years as a Parish Councillor, including twelve months as its Chairman.

After Lady Margaret's death Stanton Court lay empty, accumulating months of wartime dust, until it was sold in 1951 and another turning point in its history began.

9
No Gymnastics in the Drawing Room

Sweltering in the tropical heat Kenneth King made his way down to the shoreline where the air was cooler. Sitting down for a rest he turned to gaze back over the rubber plantation. Soon he would be leaving the Cameroons and returning to England, where a rural life with his young family beckoned, only this time, unlike his customary annual sojourns, he would be going back to Stanton Court for good.

With the death of Lady Margaret Spicer in 1949, Stanton Court passed briefly into the hands of two local landowners, Clifford Drewett and Harold Smith, before being sold in 1951 to Kenneth and Gywneth King.

Kenneth King spent his working life as a senior superintendent of rubber plantations in Malaya and West Africa. Every year he would take two months annual leave to escape the monsoons and would return to England. It was during one of these trips that he seized upon the opportunity to buy Stanton Court and its estate, seeing it as both an investment and as the place where he would spend his retirement, although it was to be another ten years before he settled in Stanton Court permanently.

Rubber plantation in the Cameroons (Gillian Howard)

WILTSHIRE

In the heart of the Beaufort Hunt.
4½ miles from the market town of Chippenham (London 90 minutes).

Picturesque Small Residential Estate

known as

STANTON COURT

Suite of 4 magnificent reception rooms all panelled in old Tudor style, 10 principle bedrooms, 3 luxurious bathrooms, well-arranged domestic offices.

Co.'s electric light. Central heating. Garages. Stables. Charming garden and walks, parklands. 3 good Cottages.

Extending in all to **ABOUT 12 ACRES**

TO BE SOLD BY AUCTION ON MAY 4, 1951

Particulars from the Solicitors: Messrs. GOLDING, HARGROVE AND PALMER, 98, Cannon Street, London, E.C.4. or the Auctioneers: Messrs. TILLEY & CULVERWELL, Chippenham, Wiltshire, and Messrs. POWLETT & FLOYD, Bath, Somerset.

Country Life *advertisement, 1951 (A. Adams)*

In the interim the Kings set about dividing the Court into flats as a way of generating income, and appointed a caretaker to oversee the property. In the early years after the War this would have been the most viable option as there was more demand for smaller properties and building materials were in short supply.

An aerial view of Stanton Court taken in 1951 shows a large estate extending east as far as Kington Lane and encompassing land where Court Gardens now stands. The high wall, bordering the main village street, which extended to Kington Lane still remains to this day. Running due south from the stables were tennis courts, and south of these to the ha-ha was a high Cotswold stone wall, bordering a field, with impressive pineapple finials on its gates. This imposing structure was taken down and the finials removed when the land was sold for new development in 1985.

The school, which then consisted of one classroom, can be seen opposite the stable block and the central tower of the church and roof of the Manor can just be glimpsed through the trees. In the days before the motorway, the Court was surrounded on three sides by extensive farmland whilst the aerodrome is visible quite clearly to the North.

Initially the Court was divided into eight flats plus Stables Cottage – there were three flats occupying the central part of the Court, one on each floor; two flats in the West wing, and three flats in the North and East wings, (two on the ground floor and one on the first floor). At some stage during the

Aerial view of Stanton Court in 1951 (Howard collection)

North wall with greenhouses, 1950 (Howard collection)

1960s the first floor flat of North Wing was accessed via an external staircase adjoining the courtyard.

In the post War years Stanton Court was a rambling austere property, fuelled by coal burning stoves in the days before central heating. Tenants to the flats in the West Wing and central Court would enter the property via the main central front door, and pass the communal telephone in the hallway before turning either right through what is now a dining room into West Wing, left into what is now a kitchen, but was then a bedroom, or continuing upstairs.

East wall with pineapple finials, 1950 (Howard collection)

Four views of the interior of Flat 4 in 1966 (Howard collection)

Stables Cottage at this time consisted of a kitchen and bathroom downstairs, and two bedrooms upstairs, adjoining a hayloft and tack room. This was later converted together with the stables and garages in the late 1970s and early 1980s to Stables Cottage and the Coach House.

Many of the tenants who came to live in Stanton Court in the 1950s and 60s were from the Royal Air Force. By 1951 the population of Stanton St. Quintin had risen to 1,184 (from 259 in 1931), necessitating the building of more housing. Five service houses had been built at Blenheim Gardens in 1936 and a further ten were added in 1951. Forty-three service houses were built in Valetta Gardens between 1950 and 1951, and many residents also lived on the base.

Rear of Stables Cottage (Howard collection)

With the sharp influx of residents to the village it soon became apparent that the village school, with its single Victorian classroom, was not big enough to accommodate the needs of the village schoolchildren. In order to appreciate what happened next in terms of the changing status of the village school, and the role of Stanton Court it is perhaps helpful to consider a brief history of how the school evolved.

An educational establishment had existed in the village since the early 19th century, when Rev. Grey Cotes started a small school in the chancel of the church in 1827. Six years later a daily school for 25-30 children was begun on a site now occupied by School Cottage, and this was supported by the Earl of Radnor and Rev. Grey Cotes, although tuition was paid for by the parents.

The Church School Enquiry of 1846/7 records that the population of the parish at that time was 302, and there were 41 pupils in day school and 13 in Sunday school. At that time School Cottage was divided into two with the schoolroom and the teacher's house taking up the west side and east side respectively.

In 1849 a new schoolroom, which still exists today as the reception classroom, was built on to the West side of School Cottage. It was paid for by Viscount Folkestone, Earl of Radnor, Rev. Grey Cotes and the Church and was designated a Church of England School, although it was owned by the Radnor family. The patronage of the school by the Radnor family continued until 1922, when the trustees of the will of Meredith Meredith Brown of Stanton Manor sold the school to local trustees, the Rector and two others.

In 1952 the Education Authority wrote to the School Managers giving them notice that during 1953-54 100 extra children were expected to attend the village school, mostly from the Air Ministry quarters, and the wheels were set in motion to build a large extension. In the meantime the managers were asked to consider using the Church Hall as an extra classroom, but this was rejected on account of the distance and the lack of space for tables and chairs, and instead use was made of 49 Stanton St. Quintin and the large drawing room and grounds at Stanton Court.

Whilst a temporary transfer of school premises to Stanton Court was underway, work began on an extension to the school, built by the County Council, with the proviso that once completed, the school would change status from a Voluntary Controlled Church School to a County Primary School.

And so it was after the long summer holiday of 1952, that junior pupils returning to Stanton St. Quintin School for a new term found themselves having lessons in the oak panelled drawing room and dining room at Stanton Court, whilst the infants were schooled at the cottage at no.49. Both juniors and infants would meet up at lunchtime, when they would dine in the North Wing at Stanton Court where Mrs. Anstee and Mrs. Drew served lunch in two sittings.

The schoolroom at Stanton Court (A. Smith)

Mrs. Elizabeth (Bessie) Anstee was also employed as the school cleaner, whilst her husband Bernard, who had himself been a pupil at the school, was for many years the school boiler man.

Mrs. Anstee remembers the large drawing room at Stanton Court (which was later divided into two rooms by the Kings) with its fireplace at each end containing slow combustion stoves and she also remembers varnishing the wooden floors.

Whilst the classes were underway on the ground floor, Stanton Court was still occupied by tenants on the upper floors. In October 1953 some of the tenants objected to the noise of the piano, so the Church Hall was hired for two afternoons per week for singing, games and dancing and the following notice went up in the Court:

TERMS FOR TENANCY OF ROOM AT STANTON COURT
Tenants to be allowed use of room between 8.30am and 4.30pm during the school year
Tenants to be allowed use of cloakroom outside this drawing room.
No gymnastics, singing, musical or classes of a nature that will disturb the tenants of the various flats to be allowed.
Tenants to provide their own cleaner
Children to be taken in and out of the room and to use the premises under the supervision of a responsible School teacher.
The room not to be used for meals at any time.
Approach to the room to be made through the side entrance by the cloakroom.

Fifty years later, the sound of the piano can once again be heard through the French window and the garden is a frequently used backdrop for displays of amateur gymnastics!

In September 1954 the new school building opened, which now consisted of three classrooms, a hall, kitchen, cloakrooms and office space.

Opening of the new school building, 1954. Pictured are Mrs. Kay, headmistress (standing), Mrs. Hankey (third from left), Rev. Frank Day (far right) (E. Gibb)

Mrs. Kay had been appointed as an assistant teacher at the school in January 1953 but when the new school opened she took up the position of headmistress, and she too became a tenant at Stanton Court, occupying the top floor flat with her family. Her daughter, Maureen, remembers the top floor flat as being rather a spooky place, particularly at night when the floorboards creaked and the water tanks would make strange noises in the dark. However living there had its bonuses and it was shortly after she came to live in Stanton St. Quintin with her mother that Maureen met and married David Smith of Cook's Farm.

Mrs. Kay, headmistress, with her grandson Neil in 1958 (M. Smith)

The Rector of St. Giles during this time was Rev. Frank Day. He became incumbent in 1952 when his predecessor Rev. Francois de Chaumont died suddenly whilst on holiday.

In 1954 the benefice of Stanton St. Quintin was held in plurality with Seagry. Rev. Day resigned in 1959 to become Rector of Grittleton with Leigh Delamere and Rev. Lake became Rector of St. Giles. On Rev. Lake's death in 1964 services at St. Giles were conducted by Padre W.L. O'Neill from RAF Hullavington, then in May 1965 Rev. Day, who was still Rector of Grittleton, was appointed priest in charge of Stanton. An Order of Council in December 1967 created the new United Benefice of Stanton St. Quintin and Grittleton with Leigh Delamere, and Rev. Day was instituted for his second turn in 1968. Rev. Day was responsible for compiling an information booklet for visitors to St. Giles in which he stated that his years there as Rector had been the most happy in his memory.

Included in his notes on the church he states that the churchyard closed in 1899 and from 1954 became an expense on the parish rates. The extension across the road, adjoining the school, was opened in 1898 and at the time of writing – 1965 – the Church Council was seeking more ground, an issue which continues to vex the Parish Council forty years later!

Kenneth King with his daughters, Philippa and Gillian, and a friend, 1958 (Howard collection)

In 1961 Kenneth King took early retirement and came back to England. He and his wife Gywneth and their three children, Gillian, Philippa and Peter, who had boarded at Grittleton School whilst their parents lived abroad, would spend most of the next twenty years living at Stanton Court, apart from a brief spell between 1962 and 1963 when they lived at Nettleton.

Sitting room at Stanton Court (Howard collection)

At Stanton Court the Kings occupied the ground floor flat in the central part of the house, and made several alterations to the layout of the rooms. The double sided oak staircase in the entrance hall had been walled in on one side in the 1950s, creating an additional room which they made into a bedroom, with a single high window. The large oak panelled drawing room was divided two-thirds of the way across and the smaller of the two resulting rooms was made into a kitchen. An additional kitchen was built on the first floor, in the small utility corridor adjoining East Wing.

Gill Howard vividly remembers her mother owning a Norwegian tapestry which she had been using inadvertently as a floor mat until she came across a similar tapestry sold at auction for a substantial sum of money. The Norwegian

Mrs. Gwyneth King with Gillian, Philippa and Peter, 1959 (Howard collection)

tapestry subsequently exchanged hands for a similar sum and this went towards refurbishing the tennis courts which existed south of Stables Cottage.

The south-facing terrace ran the whole length of the house in those days from the West Wing to Stables Cottage. Sadly the Wellingtonia tree so fondly remembered by the Cannan children in the 1930s, was taken down in 1959 when it was destroyed by lightning, and the Kings subsequently installed lightning conductors on the roof.

During their time at the Court the Kings put fruit trees in the orchards and erected the potting shed and greenhouse. Gill also remembers as a child hiding in the old oak tree and painting in the spinney.

In 1977 the deeds of Stanton Court show that the property was once more converted from eight flats to four houses which now became Stanton Court, West Wing, East Wing and North Wing. Within the next couple of years the property was sold in divided lots and Stanton Court entered another phase in its history.

The Wellingtonia tree in 1959 (top); the Wellingtonia stump, with Gwyneth and Peter King, 1965 (above) (Howard collection)

10

All the Kings' Courtiers

'Home, in one form or another, is the great object of life.'
Josiah Gilbert Holland

The Kings were the last family to own Stanton Court as a whole estate and gradually, after nearly thirty years as landlords, they began the process of dividing up the property and selling it. In 1962 they sold fourteen plots of land adjoining the main village road and Kington Lane and this later led to the housing development known as Court Gardens. In 1977 they were granted planning permission to convert Stanton Court from eight flats back to four self-contained units, and these reverted to West Wing, Stanton Court, East Wing and North Wing. As it happened amongst the first of the new property owners were some of the next generation of the King family.

In 1979 the King's eldest daughter Gill, and her husband, Jim Howard, bought Stables Cottage and the building adjoining it containing garages, and set about renovating the former. Meanwhile the previous year Gill's cousin John Barrett and his partner Janet Morgan bought the East Wing and renamed it Stanton Lodge, and the West Wing was sold to Roger Pope who moved from Yatton Keynell.

Gill Howard had spent a large part of her childhood at Stanton Court, and now it became home to her three daughters Laurie, Martha and Beth. (Later when the family moved to Nailsworth their son, Max, was born). She recalls living in most of the flats at Stanton Court at some stage during the conversion process and remembers that, in the absence of central heating, it was invariably draughty and freezing cold! Whilst renovations were underway at Stables Cottage the family lived for a short time in the top floor flat at Stanton Court.

Jim Howard, who was in the building trade, made several improvements to Stanton Court during the Seventies, including the introduction of central heating. Other alterations involved converting the ground floor bedroom adjacent to the oak staircase into a kitchen, which remains to this day. Part of this conversion involved removing Bertrand Bouverie's fireplace in 1984, and this was sold for £2000. Another window was also added to the room, between the kitchen and the front corridor, supplementing the single high window which until then had made the room fairly dark and gloomy, and the large glass fronted cupboards were added.

Peter King in 1964, outside the garages which were later converted to the Coach House (Howard collection)

The back door of the Court was altered at this time from one which was East facing to one which was South facing, allowing the owners of Stanton Lodge greater privacy. A double garage was added adjacent to the front wall of Stanton Court in 1979 which, it later transpired, was over the site of the old underground ice house long since redundant. In 1981 the Howards began renovating the Coach House and shortly afterwards sold it to Mr. and Mrs. Eric Wilding.

Stanton Court, 1964. The buildings to the left were converted to Stables Cottage, and those on the right to the Coach House (Howard collection)

Incorporated into the new Coach House were three integral garages which over the years have changed ownership amongst the occupiers of Coach House, Stables Cottage and North Wing. At the time of writing, two are owned by the occupants of Stables Cottage but leased to North Wing, and the third is owned by the Coach House.

In the West Wing the front corridor to the right of the central entrance was blocked off and converted into a kitchen. Prior to this there had been a ground floor kitchen overlooking the rock garden, facing West and a first floor kitchen facing South over the back garden, however these were now removed.

Kenneth and Gwyneth King retained North Wing until 1982 when it was then sold to Caedmon and Helen Featherston (Appendix 2 details the conveyancing of the properties.) When Kenneth King died in 1983 the central part of the house, Stanton Court, passed to the Howards who sold it to Alfie and Marilyn Smith in 1985.

The Smiths, who hailed from Great Somerford, both worked long hours and as a result they engaged the help of a young nanny, Sarah Miles, who lived in and who helped look after their young daughter Lucy. Sarah recalls that the interior of the house then bore little resemblance to the house today.

In the eighties a large glass door partition was built at the top of the stairs on the first floor landing effectively isolating the top floor flat. This was occupied for a short while in 1987 by Gerald and Shirley Cooper who were friends of the Smiths.

A first floor store cupboard used to block access to the back staircase but this was later removed in the nineties and no doubt was a necessity to comply with fire regulations when the property was used as bed and breakfast accommodation.

On the ground floor the room to the right of the entrance hall, which is currently a dining room, was used by Marilyn Smith as an office, the fireplace in the large sitting room was removed and replaced by a wood burning stove and a considerable amount of sitting room floor space was taken up by a large grand piano. Outside, Gandhi the goose presided over the garden, and a pond in the wood, together with several cats and guinea pigs.

Sarah, Lucy's nanny, was married in 1989 with Lucy as her bridesmaid, and shortly afterwards the Smiths made plans to emigrate to New Zealand. During her time at the Court, Sarah made friends with Jo Gingell, who was

Aerial view of Stanton Court in the early 1990s (Anne and Paul Adams)

employed as a nanny to Kevin and Ann Gilbert, who in 1986 came to live in the West Wing. Twenty years later she was delighted to make a chance encounter with Jo once again on a trip back to the Court, as Jo moved back to the West Wing in 2005 to live with her partner Paul and their young family.

Ann Gilbert bought the West Wing in 1986 after it had lain empty for twelve months following the departure of Phil and Pam Iles to the USA. Ann worked in London and had been looking for a country bolt hole for some time. Although, by her own admission, she was not immediately attracted to the house which appeared quite dark and gloomy, she did see enormous potential in the large garden and its proximity to St. Giles Church; and shortly after taking up residence there she married Kevin in the parish church, followed by a reception in a marquee on the lawn.

In 1990 the Smiths emigrated to New Zealand and sold Stanton Court to Paul and Anne Adams. A multi-talented family, the Adams turned their hand to many projects within the Court and involved themselves in the community, resurrecting amongst other things the tradition of holding an annual village fête in the garden. Inside the house, the Adams removed the double doors at the top of the stairs and installed an additional en suite bathroom for one of the first floor bedrooms. They also repaired the roof and renovated the wood panelling. Anne, who had a flair for interior design, made many of the soft furnishings which exist in the Court today and for a while Stanton Court was a popular location for tourist accommodation. Ten years after the Adams' departure, requests for bed and breakfast are still received on a regular basis by the current owners!

Overlapping with the Adams' tenure of the Court were Keith and Audrey Galpin who bought the East Wing in 1992. It had reverted to East Wing, formerly Stanton Lodge, in the 1980s, but the Galpins now re-named it ' The Old Pantry', the name currently in existence.

The Galpins had bought their property from Mark and Jane Humphreys, who had lived there for 2 years with their young sons. Prior to that the East Wing had been occupied by a tenant called Annette who worked in an art gallery in London. Annette was the first to install a burglar alarm in the village to protect the valuable paintings at the Court (sadly long since gone!).

The Galpins were very keen gardeners and lovingly tended their extensive garden. Shortly after they moved in 1999 Keith excavated two massive Bath stone water tanks under the gravel drive between the Old Pantry and North

The rainwater tanks found between North Wing and the Old Pantry (Keith Galpin)

Wing, which were reserve rain water tanks and were probably in existence in Bertrand Bouverie's time.

In 1994 Stanton Court became a listed building. Two years later Peter and Fiona Baskett bought Stanton Court and would see the house through to the next Millennium.

11
The New Millennium

'The ornament of a house is the friends who frequent it.'
Ralph Waldo Emerson

Anyone who has ever lived at Stanton Court will tell you that they have happy memories of the place. Another trait that successive owners have shared in common is a strong sense of stewardship, a responsibility to preserve the environs of Stanton Court for future generations. This was demonstrated to my husband, Peter, and me, when as prospective new occupants we met the villagers at a social gathering before we moved here. Several members of the party spoke fondly of the time when they had been pupils in the long oak panelled drawing room, many remembered playing hide-and-seek in the garden, and others were quick to remind us of the long held tradition of holding village fêtes in the garden!

The village fête, that quintessentially summer occasion, as traditional and English as a Victoria sponge, has been celebrated on many occasions at Stanton Court over the past two hundred years. From the mid-nineteenth century, when the Rectory gardens of Fanny Grey Cotes were compared to a 'Turkish carpet', to the Depression when the proceeds of Lady Margaret's fêtes were divided between the church and the families of Welsh miners, the village fête has always been a genial occasion and one which, like our predecessors the Adams, we were happy to continue.

Although the annual fêtes have had slight variations in theme from year to year, such as a red, white and blue party to celebrate Queen Elizabeth II's

Golden Jubilee, and a Millennium party, the choir, the tombola, the silent auction and the pavlovas were as consistent, familiar and welcome a sight as a comfortable pair of old slippers. The author would also take particular delight in the fact that one day every year she would become an official licensee for the day!

In 1937, the year of King George VI's coronation, the profits of the village fête were £115, which went towards distempering the church roof and providing dorsal and riddal curtains. In 2003, the proceeds of Stanton Court Village Lunch exceeded £1400, and this was divided between St. Giles Church and Stanton St. Quintin School.

The village fête, choir and party for HM Queen Elizabeth's Golden Jubilee (above, left and opposite page) (author)

Stanton Court is a house which provides a most conducive environment for a good party and there have been many occasions to celebrate in recent years.

One such memorable occasion in our early days here was the wedding blessing of our good friends Drs. Mike and Cynthia Parr on 1st March 1997, at which Rev. John Morgan officiated. Two months earlier they had married in Sydney, Australia and were grateful for the opportunity to renew their vows at St. Giles Church in the presence of family and friends who had been unable to

travel so far afield. The reception was held next door at Stanton Court with the catering provided by Philip and Elizabeth Bullock of Stanton Manor Hotel, (some of which was carried ably through the graveyard whilst the ceremony was in progress). Emotions ran high that day, not least because many of the Celtic guests were able to watch, in an adjoining television room, Scotland defeat Ireland 38–10 in the rugby international at Murrayfield.

When our daughter Beatrice was baptised at St. Giles Church, once again Rev. John Morgan conducted the ceremony. Also in attendance was Daisy, our golden Labrador, who had followed guests surreptitiously from our open front door through to the church in a scene reminiscent of seventy years earlier when Chips, the Sealyham terrier would join the congregation. However, unlike Chips who would join in with the hymn singing, Daisy sat quietly at the back of the church throughout the ceremony then dutifully followed everyone as they filed out to Stanton Court to join in the party.

Family pets have always featured highly at Stanton Court. Photographs throughout the past 100 years have usually sported the ubiquitous black Labrador, whether it be Jill in 1931 or Pongo in 2005. Nobby and Bramble, the ponies, were a familar sight in the 1960s as was Gandhi the goose in the 1980s. Today it is the farmer's ponies Spice and Macduff who are often seen grazing in our field adjoining the wood. The wood and orchards also provide a cosy habitat for many squirrels, moles, badgers and rabbits, and occasionally we catch a glimpse of a fox illuminated late at night by the garden lights. In the garden of West Wing, adjoining the churchyard, is a pet cemetery, with stone wall plaques commemorating the lives of Dinah, Wicklow, Chips and Ivy, beloved four legged

Nobby and Bramble, 1966 (Howard collection)

Beatrice Baskett and Amelia Rosser inspect the Pet Cemetery, West Wing, 2005 (author)

friends who frequented Stanton Court in the 1920s and 30s. When Daisy, the golden Labrador, died in 2002 we planted a hawthorn tree in her memory in the orchard, which flowers every May around the anniversary of her death.

The orchards, which were originally planted by the Kings in the 1950s, reap bountiful supplies of apples and plums every year, more than enough to garnish Harvest festivals, furnish freezers and fill guests with plum tarts and apple crumbles many times over.

The arboretum continues to grow. In addition to the solid old oak tree which has stood for hundreds of years, the wood at the bottom of the garden, begun after the Cannan's time in the 1930s, has flourished, and with the new millennium several more young trees such as acers and beech trees have been added. It is a garden which Fanny Grey Cotes would have difficulty recognising but one of which I'm sure she would be proud.

The Baskett family continue to delight in hosting social functions at Stanton Court whether for neighbours and courtiers or for guests from all over the world and will usually recognise the occasion by hoisting an appropriate flag in their

The old oak tree becomes Owl's House for the day at a children's party, 2005 (author)

Peter in the wine cellar (S.Davies)

honour from the red and gold banner of Northumbria, the five-pointed stars of Singapore, to the maple leaf of Canada.

One occasion when guests clocked up many miles to be here was a surprise birthday party for Peter. As local guests sipped champagne on the lawn to the sound of a jazz band and calypso steel drums, the Canadian contingent of the family cycled down the yew avenue on an old fashioned ice cream cart. It was one of the few occasions when the main guest (and co-host) was rendered speechless!

After hundreds of years the symbiotic relationship between

Fiona, Beatrice and Peter by the goldfish pond (S. Davies)

Stanton Court and Stanton Manor continues. The original Manor House, described by Aubrey and Jackson, was taken down in 1856 and replaced by a large stone farmhouse. In 1920 the Radnor family sold the estate, which at that time consisted of 335 acres of land plus Manor farmhouse, to Basil Hankey. One year before his wife Maud's death in 1972 most of the farm land was sold to Mr. R. Deeley, who in 1983 sold it to his son-in-law and daughter Mr. and Mrs. Lesley Plummer, and their two sons Richard and Ian continue to farm the land to this day. In 1972 the farmhouse was sold separately and in 1989 it became Stanton Manor Hotel.

Stanton Manor Hotel in 2005 (author)

During our time at Stanton Court the hotel has changed hands several times from Philip and Elizabeth Bullock, to Duncan and Linda Hickling, to the present owners Robert and Linda Davies. All have been most gracious and co-operative in hosting events in tandem with Stanton Court, whether providing catering for a wedding or accommodation for doctors from all over Europe, as part of the European Resuscitation Council Educator course, or a dinner venue for the medical officers at Castle Combe race circuit.

Sometimes Peter and I have been credited unwittingly for their enterprise, such as the time when we were hosting a dinner for the local branch of the Royal Army Medical Corps and guests temporarily interrupted their meal to view the impressive firework display they thought we had laid on for them. Little did they know that it had been specifically provided for the wedding reception which was in progress next door.

We feel privileged to live in close proximity to the Church, which has played so important a role in all of our lives and provides a spiritual and crucial community focus for many villagers. The new millennium has brought more changes to the Church and in 2006 St. Giles is one of eight parish churches in the Gauzebrook Area Ministry.

Stanton Court at the beginning of the 21st century is an imposing Grade II listed building divided into six private residences. To the West it is shaded by the yew trees of the Norman churchyard of St. Giles, the most tangible clue linking the Court to its former glory as a rectory. To the North and East lie the school and houses of the little village of Stanton St. Quintin which, although rural in many aspects, serves as a small commuter community for many residents. This notion of a transient population is further reinforced by the

The author (centre) with John Cannan and his sister Helen McAlpine, 2005 (Peter Baskett)

presence of the M4 motorway two fields away to the South of the house, providing a consistent background hum akin to the sound of a distant seashore. Other sound effects familiar to this contemporary rural idyll include the soft drones of Hercules aircraft on their sorties from RAF Lyneham or the occasional swish of an overhead glider from nearby Hullavington airfield.

As for Stanton Court, the Wellingtonia tree has long since disappeared but the warmth and conviviality continues, and like so many before us we are proud to be Courtiers.

Appendix 1
Incumbency of the Parish of St Giles, 1296 – 1780

	Patron	*Rector*
1296		Matthew Hamme (Vicar)
1302	Hubert de St. Quentin	Edgar de Wyly (Rector)
1311	Hubert de St. Quentin	William de Chiryton
1322	Hubert de St. Quentin	Hugo de Chausey
1342	Hubert de St. Quentin	William de Starenton
1349	John de Farle	John de Farle
1381	John de St. Quentin	Hugh Vaughan
1384	John de St. Quentin	Richard Pyerwight
1391	Hugh Tybbe	Hugh Tybbe
1397	Henry Fitzhugh (dominus de Ravenswath)	Nicholas Yatting
1401	Henry Fitzhugh (dominus de Ravenswath)	John Flygnt (Fygnt)
1406	Henry Fitzhugh (dominus de Ravenswath)	Nicholas Sterre
1414	Henry Fitzhugh (dominus de Ravenswath)	Rev. Butle
1428	John Pygot and others	John Comleygh (Comely)
1439	Fitzhugh dominus de Stanton Quentin	John Godystone
1479	Alice —	Thomas Sutton
1489	Alice —	WilliamTymson
1507	His Majesty the King	John Smart
1555	Sir Henry Long	William Augustine
1574	John Dannes and Rober Franklyn	William Jones
1609	His Majesty the King (per lapsum)	Robert Merrick
1639	James Charmbury	William Charmbury
1677	Sir Giles Hungerford	John Byrom
1717	Robert Lexington	William Twentyman
1732	Sir Edward de Bouverie of Langford	—Powell
1759	Jacob Folkestone	John Shergold
1778	Jacob, Earl of Radnor	Edward Moore (resigned)

For later patrons and incumbents see the table on page 34.

Appendix 2
Conveyancing of Stanton Court from 1951-2005

1951 Clifford Drewett and Harold Smith sell Stanton Court to Kenneth and Gywneth King

1962 14 plots of land, having a frontage to the main road of the village and to the road leading to Kington St. Michael, sold by the Kings to William Kew. **Court Gardens** created on this site with the building of 12 bungalows along Kington Lane and adjoining cul de sac.

1977 The Kings apply successfully to convert 8 flats into 4 self contained units.

Stables Cottage

1979 Sold by the Kings to Jim and Gillian Howard

1984 John and Hilary Evans become the new owners, and in **1986** extend the premises by adding a lounge, porch and cloakroom.

1989 Brian and Fiona Chapman

1994 Peter and Clare White

2001 Lucy Bradnam

2002 Tim and Marina Cowan

East Wing

1979 The Kings sell East Wing to John Barrett and Janet Morgan who rename it **Stanton Lodge**

1985 Mark and Jane Humphreys- Stanton Lodge reverts to the East Wing

1992 Keith and Audrey Galpin move in and re- name it "**The Old Pantry**"

1999 Michael and Kate Harrison

2003 Richard and Katherine Lamb

2004 Alex and Sarah Greig

West Wing

1977 The Kings sell West Wing to Roger Pope

1981 Phil and Pam Iles

1986 Kevin and Anne Gilbert

North Wing

1982 The Kings sell North Wing to Caedmon and Helen Featherstone

1990 Richard and Pet Brown

1997 Simon and Sheila Willis

1998 John Rodda and Sally Morgan

2001 Gary and Sally Howells

2004 Nigel Fleet and Rachel Clark

The Coach House:

1978 The Kings lease 2 garages to the Howards

1982 Dorothy and Eric Wilding

1995 Ian and Sara Findlay

1996 Denis and Jeanine Goddard

Stanton Court:

Following Kenneth King's death in 1983, Gill and Jim Howard sell Stanton Court in 1985

1985 Alfred and Marilyn Smith

1990 Paul and Anne Adams

1996 Peter and Fiona Baskett

Bibliography

Sources used Throughout

Crowley, D.A., 'Stanton St. Quintin', *Victoria History of Wiltshire*, vol. 14, 1991, pp.213-21
The Parish Book by Rev. Hon. Bertrand Bouverie, continued by Basil Hankey 1877-1955 (Wiltshire & Swindon Record Office 1621/29)

1 *In the Beginning*

Society of Antiquaries: Canon Jackson Collection
Badeni, June, *Wiltshire Forefathers*, 1960
Codrington, Thomas, *Roman Roads of Britain*, 3rd ed, Sheldon Press, 1928
BBC History: Malmesbury: England's Oldest Borough
Freeman, Jane, and Watkin, Aelred (eds.) *A History of Malmesbury*, Wilts CC, 1999

2 *Debauchery, Robbery and Murder most Foul*

Parker, Derek, and Chandler, John, *Wiltshire Churches: an Illustrated History*, Sutton, 1993
Woodruffe, Brian, *Wiltshire Villages*, Hale 1982
Badeni, June, *Wiltshire Forefathers*, 1960
Aubrey, John, and Jackson. J.E. (ed.), *Wiltshire: the topographical collections*, WANHS, 1862
Wiltshire Gazette, 1923
Settle, Mary Lee, *All the Brave Promises,: the memoirs of an aircraftman 2nd class*, Heinemann, 1966

3 *A New Rectory for Stanton St. Quintin*

Foster, J. (ed), *Alumni Oxionienses*, 1715-1886, Kraus Reprint, 1968
Parochial returns made to the Select Committee appointed to enquire into the education of the poor, vol.2, p.1037 [reproduced by Elizabeth Gibb]

4 *Beneath the Weeping Willow*

Stratford, Jenny, (ed.), *Catalogue of the Jackson Collection . . . in . . . Windsor Castle*, Academic Press, 1981
Devizes and Wiltshire Gazette

5 *'Patria Cara, Carior Libertas'*

Venn, John and J.A. (ed.) *Alumni Cantabrigienses*, Thoemmes Press 2001 (reprint)
Burke's peerage, baronetage and knightage, various eds.
National Maritime Museum
Wiltshire Gazette, 1926

6 *The Cocktail Years*

Godfrey, Rupert (ed.), *Letters from a Prince,* Little Brown, 1968
Hudson, Helen, *Cumberland Lodge: a House through History,* Phillimore, 1997
Marie Louise, Princess, *My Memories of Six Reigns,* Evans Bros, 1979
Wodehouse, P.G., *Summer Lightning,* Herbert Jenkins, 1929
Smith, Angela (ed.), *150 years of Stanton St. Quintin School*

7 *Daisy Chains and Tiaras*

Wiltshire Gazette, 1928
Godfrey, Rupert (ed.), *Letters from a Prince,* Little Brown, 1968
Spicer family archives, in private possession

8 *Damp Greatcoats, Sege Blankets and Stewed Tea*

Settle, Mary Lee, *All the Brave Promises,: the memoirs of an aircraftman 2nd class,* Heinemann, 1966
Berryman, David, *Wiltshire Airfields in the Second World War,* Countryside, 2002
Smith, Angela (ed.), *150 years of Stanton St. Quintin School*
Imperial War Museum

9 *No Gymnastics in the Drawing Room*

Gibb, Elizabeth, *The parish book of Stanton St Quintin,* transcribed by E. and I. Gibb, 1990, in private possession
Smith, Angela (ed.), *150 years of Stanton St. Quintin School*

10 *All the Kings' Courtiers*

Stanton Court deeds and conveyances, in private possession

Index